English
FOR COMMON ENTRANCE

13+

Revision Guide

Susan Elkin

GALORE PARK

AN HACHETTE UK COMPANY

Acknowledgements

The Publishers would like to thank Kornel Kossuth for all his support in producing this book.

The Publishers would like to thank the following for permission to reproduce copyright material.

Acknowledgements: **p 7** Gerald Durrell: from *The Drunken Forest* (Penguin Random House Ltd.), permission sought; **p 8** Linda Newbery: from *Set in Stone* (Definitions); **p 9** John Steinbeck: from *The Red Pony* (Penguin Classics), permission sought; **p 10** Nigel Hinton: from the TV script of *Buddy* (Heinemann), permission sought; **p 11** Chris Stewart: from *Driving Over Lemons* (Sort of Books); **p 12** Frank McCourt: from *Angela's Ashes* (Harper Perennial), permission sought; **p 13** John Wyndham: from *The Day of the Triffids* (Penguin Random House), permission sought; **p 15** Frances Mayes: from *Under the Tuscan Sun* (Bantam); **p 18** Meera Syal: from *Anita and Me* (Flamingo); **p 20** Nick Stafford: from the play *War Horse*, based on the novel by Michael Morpurgo (Faber and Faber); **p 23** Alfred Noyes: from 'The Highwayman'; **p 24** Ted Hughes: from 'November' (Faber & Faber); **p 24** Walter de la Mare: from 'Silver'; **p 24** William Blake: from 'The Echoing Green'; **p 24** John Betjeman: from 'Diary of a Church Mouse' (John Murray); **p 25** Charles Causley: from 'Timothy Winters' (reproduced with permission from David Higham Associates); **p 25** W.H. Auden: from 'Roman Wall Blues'; **p 25** Geoffrey Chaucer (translated by Nevil Coghill): from *The Canterbury Tales*; **p 25** D.H. Lawrence: from 'Last Lesson of the Afternoon'; **p 25** Charles Causley: from 'Cowboy Song' (reproduced with permission from David Higham Associates); **p 26** Hal Summers: from 'Out of School' (Oxford University Press); **p 26** Stevie Smith: from 'Not Waving but Drowning' (Faber & Faber); **p 29** Seamus Heaney: from 'Follower' (Faber & Faber); **p 30** Irene McLeod: from 'Lone Dog'; **p 31** Laurie Lee: from 'Sunken Evening'; **p 34** Michael Wright: from a letter to the *Telegraph*; **p 35** Roald Dahl: from *Charlie and the Chocolate Factory* (Puffin); **p 36** Susan Elkin: from 'Delusions of Grandeur', published by *The Independent*; Paul Vincent: from a letter to the *Telegraph* **p 37** John Humphrys: from *Beyond Words* (Hodder Paperbacks); **p 45** Michael Morpurgo: from *Best Mates* (HarperCollins Children's Books); **p 46** Rosemary Sutcliff: from *The Eagle of the Ninth* (Oxford University Press); **p 47** Tanya Landman: from *Apache* (Copyright © 2007 Tanya Landman, reproduced with permission of Walker Books Ltd); **p 52** Richard Adams: from *Watership Down* (Puffin Classics); **p 53** Mary Hooper: from *The Disgrace of Kitty Grey* (Bloomsbury Classics); **p 53** Simon Packham: from *Firewallers* (Piccadilly Press); **p 61** Ernest Hemingway: from 'Indian Camp' in *The Snows of Kilimanjaro* (Simon & Schuster); **p 62** Linda Newbery: from *Set in Stone* (Black Swan); **p 63** Jay Black: from *Urban Outlaws Counterstrike* (Bloomsbury Childrens).

Every effort has been made to trace all copyright holders, but if any have been inadvertently overlooked, the Publishers will be pleased to make the necessary arrangements at the first opportunity.

Although every effort has been made to ensure that website addresses are correct at time of going to press, Galore Park cannot be held responsible for the content of any website mentioned in this book. It is sometimes possible to find a relocated web page by typing in the address of the home page for a website in the URL window of your browser.

Hachette UK's policy is to use papers that are natural, renewable and recyclable products and made from wood grown in sustainable forests. The logging and manufacturing processes are expected to conform to the environmental regulations of the country of origin.

Orders: please contact Bookpoint Ltd, 130 Park Drive, Milton Park, Abingdon, Oxon OX14 4SE. Telephone: (44) 01235 827720. Fax: (44) 01235 400454. Email education@bookpoint.co.uk Lines are open from 9 a.m. to 5 p.m., Monday to Saturday, with a 24-hour message answering service. Visit our website at www.galorepark.co.uk for details of other revision guides for Common Entrance, examination papers and Galore Park publications.

ISBN: 978 1 4718 7431 4

© Susan Elkin 2016

First published in 2016 by
Galore Park Publishing Ltd,
An Hachette UK Company
Carmelite House
50 Victoria Embankment
London EC4Y 0DZ

www.galorepark.co.uk

Impression number   10 9 8 7 6 5 4 3 2 1

Year   2020 2019 2018 2017 2016

Typeset in India

Printed in Spain

A catalogue record for this title is available from the British Library.

Contents

Introduction

This book leads the pupil, teacher and parent through the preparation for the Common Entrance 13+ exam in English set by the Independent Schools Examinations Board.

It can, of course, be used independently by the pupil. It is also designed to help teachers leading revision in a classroom by providing advice and information to share, along with plenty of sample tasks to practise. Equally there is a great deal here to support the parent helping his or her child at home.

Revision can be dull. But it need not be. Everything in this book is as fresh and exciting as I know how to make it. English, with all those fantastic words, books and ideas, is a great joy.

Preparing for an exam in English should enhance pleasure in the subject not diminish it. Happy revising!

A note to parents

It may be a very long time since you studied English yourself. Perhaps you have forgotten some of the finer points. I sympathise. I'm afraid I have 'lost' most of the maths I must once have known and I find my ignorance quite embarrassing sometimes.

Chapter 6 of this book offers a very quick guide to grammar, punctuation and spelling. If, however, you still feel you're on shaky ground and want to boost your confidence, I recommend *Grammar for Grown Ups* by Katherine Fry and Rowena Kirton, published by Square Peg, 2012. You could also try *Help Your Kids With Spelling and Grammar* by Carol Vorderman (Dorling Kindersley, 2013), and *Oxford A-Z of Grammar and Punctuation* by John Seely (OUP, 2013).

Susan Elkin, July 2016

1 Approaching the exam

1.1 How to use this book

This is not a textbook. It is a revision book to help you in the last few months and weeks before you take your senior school entrance exams in Year 8 at 13+.

Its purpose is to remind you of all you have learnt in English lessons and to show you how to write good answers.

Probably, by now, you have already done quite a lot of work from textbooks. This will have widened your knowledge and understanding of English – such a lovely subject with all those delicious words and opportunities to read extensively.

Revision – which comes from Latin and means 'looking again' – is just that. You need to spend time looking back at all you have learnt so that you can show the examiner just how much you now understand, know and can do.

> This is a good time to sort out all those little grammar points that you still make mistakes with such as when to use 'its' and 'it's' or how to use 'me' and 'I' correctly. There is help with this in Chapter 6.

There are no facts to memorise in English. It is different from subjects like history, geography or science. The exam tests your ability to read perceptively, and to write well and accurately. It examines the skills which you have developed through class work.

This book builds on everything you have learnt until now and shows you how to do your best in the exam. It also provides quick reminders of the grammar, punctuation and spelling you have already been taught, as well as the technical terms you need when you are writing about English literature.

Your 13+ English exam will involve two papers and four tasks. In this book we cover first the reading tasks, then the writing tasks. In the exam, the papers and tasks will appear as outlined on page 2.

 Revision tip

As you work through the chapters – if this is your own copy of the book – you might find it helpful and encouraging to tick off the sections as you complete them. You can also make notes in the book, if you find this useful, or you can keep a revision notebook to chart your learning.

1.2 The syllabus and your exams

You will know by now what your exams involve. But, to ensure that you are quite clear about it, look carefully at the summary that follows on page 2 so that you know exactly what you will be asked to do.

Paper 1

Section A: Comprehension exercise on a passage from a novel, a play, a(n) (auto)biography or a piece of travel writing
    AND
Section B: An essay on a non-fiction topic. There are at least five questions to choose from, two of which will ask you to write about a book or books you have read. (1 hour 15 minutes, which includes planning time. 50 marks: 25 marks for Section A and 25 marks for Section B)

Paper 2

Section A: Comprehension exercise on a poem
    AND
Section B: An imaginative, descriptive or narrative composition – a story, for example, on a subject you choose from at least four options on the paper (1 hour 15 minutes, which includes planning time. 50 marks: 25 marks for Section A and 25 marks for Section B)

Levels 1 and 2

Both 13+ Common Entrance papers are offered at two levels. Level 1 is a foundation level and Level 2 is a standard level.
    Both papers will use the same passage or poem for comprehension but:

● at Level 1 the passage may be abridged so that it's slightly shorter and more difficult words may be explained

● the questions are different at each level. Level 1 questions offer the candidate more guidance than Level 2 questions.

The writing tasks on both papers are the same for each level.
    In this book we give examples of comprehension passage questions at both levels and show you ways of tackling them.

What are the examiners looking for?

The people marking your papers hope to see three main things. They want to see that you can:

● read substantial passages unaided and give independent written responses to questions requiring a range of comprehension skills

● write original creative work in the limited time the exam allows you

● use language for practical purposes, which may include responding to books you've read on your own or in class.

It is a good idea to keep these three things in mind as you revise and while you are writing your exam answers.

1.3 How to revise

Find a quiet place in which to revise. Few of us can do our best work and thinking when there is a lot of distracting background noise.
    Organise your revision so that you do at least half an hour every second day. If you revise some English for a short time regularly you will probably have worked pretty thoroughly through what you need to know.
    Don't try to revise the whole of one subject before you move on to another. That way some subjects are bound to get left until it's too late and will then have to be hurried. You might also have forgotten, by exam time, some of the work you did at the beginning. Aim to keep all your subjects evenly 'on the boil'.

Revision tip

At home, use your bedroom or some other peaceful spot for revision. At school, the library may be best.

Don't force yourself to work for hours without a break. Stop for five minutes at least once every half hour. Research about how people learn has shown that most people absorb more if they do this. Spend your break usefully – some physical exercise is particularly good for refreshing the brain with oxygen.

Promise yourself a little treat when the exams are over and you can stop revising – perhaps an exciting book which you have been looking forward to reading or a film you want to watch. This helps to put you in a better frame of mind for revision.

Make the most of all the expertise and talent available to you in school. If you really don't understand something, it's sometimes worth asking a teacher other than your own. Every teacher has his or her own way of explaining things and we all learn in different ways. You may find that suddenly you understand something which has always given you trouble.

Use past papers to familiarise yourself with the format of the exam. You will feel much more confident going into the exam if you know what to expect.

Do some physical activity every day during your revision. You will not be able to revise effectively if you are not feeling fit and well.

Eat healthy food while you are revising and don't skip meals. Your brain works better when you give it good fuel.

Make sure you read as many books as you can while you are revising to improve your own personal word bank.

If you are planning in Paper 1 to write about a text you have read, then make sure you re-read the two or three books you have studied recently, and think which you might want to write about in the exam. Remind yourself of any written work you have done on them or of notes you have made.

As you revise, practise writing paragraphs consisting of sentences of different lengths and different shapes. Notice and think about sentence length and shape while you're reading too.

Find some suitable passages from books and other places and devise your own sample papers. Then write the sort of questions based on them which you think an examiner would ask. Practise writing answers to your own questions – or swap with someone else.

Revision tip

As part of your revision, make lists of words which have more than one meaning, and useful verbs for analytical or non-fiction writing.

1.4 How to tackle the exam

Try to get a good night's sleep the night before the exam. You will be able to approach the exam much more positively if you feel refreshed. Don't eat too late the night before and have a good breakfast in the morning.

Check that you have everything you need to take into the exam. Take at least two pens in case one runs out. Your teacher will tell you if there are any other items you need to take as well.

If your school allows it, take some water into the exam with you.

Make sure you read and understand the rubric (instructions and rules) on the front of the exam paper.

Read the exam passage(s) right through carefully.

Look closely at the sentence at the top of the passage which introduces it. It's there to help you.

If the meanings of any of the words in the passage(s) are given at the bottom to help you, make sure you refer to these as you read.

Exam tip

Allow some time at the start to read and consider the questions carefully before writing anything. Don't rush into answering before you have had a chance to think about it.

Read all the questions you are asked to answer, at least twice.

Never begin to write your answers before you have read the passage(s) and the questions thoroughly.

Manage your time and check your work

Making the best use of your time is one of the most important things to get right in an exam. It can make a big difference to your marks.

For Section A allow 5 minutes to read the passage or poem and make notes. Then split the time into little blocks for each question (some answers will be shorter than others). Allow more time for a question carrying, for example, 5 or 6 marks than for a short 2-mark question. Try not to over-run on one question, leaving too little time for another. Spend no more than 25 minutes on your comprehension answers. Then spend 5 minutes checking your work.

For Section B allow 5 minutes to read the writing tasks and plan your answer. Then spend 25 minutes writing your essay. Then spend 5 minutes checking your work.

You *must* leave a few minutes at the end to double check the whole of your paper. Correct any obvious spelling mistakes. Make sure every sentence ends with a full stop. Put in any words you may have left out. Sort out any other slips you can spot. Make quick improvements where you can.

Remember to keep an eye on the clock in the room. If you don't spread your time properly across all the questions, don't finish or manage to check your work before you hand in your paper you have not shown the examiner what you can really do.

For more tips on how to get the best from your revision and exams, see *Study Skills* by Elizabeth Holtom, published by Galore Park.

★ Make sure you know

★ How to use this book.

★ The syllabus and your exams.

★ How to revise.

★ How to tackle the exam.

Literary prose comprehension

This chapter looks at the type of passage you are required to read and respond to in Paper 1 and suggests ways in which you might tackle the task. At the end of the chapter there is a full-length exam question for you to practise.

The first section of Paper 1 requires you to read a passage, or sometimes two short extracts, from a novel, play, biography, autobiography or piece of travel writing and answer questions on it.

It is your opportunity to show the examiner that you:

● can read with understanding and have a good vocabulary

● can work out what a writer is implying but not saying directly

● are able to comment on style and a writer's use of language

● can give an opinion, make a judgement or construct an argument based on what you have read

● are aware how grammar, word order and punctuation can affect meaning in writing

● can spot and explain comparisons and contrasts when you meet them in writing

● can summarise aspects of a text in your own words or using direct reference.

> Remember that in English comprehension work there are often no right or wrong answers. The main thing is that you can justify your answers.

There may be several ways of answering a question in your own words. It is your opportunity to show what and how you think. You might even spot something examiners haven't thought of. Even if it is not exactly what the examiner has written on his or her mark sheet, you will get good marks for writing something sensible and thoughtful – as long as it answers the question and you can back up what you say with evidence from the text.

2.1 Getting the basics right

Read the passage

It may sound obvious, but the first and most important thing you have to do is to read the passage through carefully. Of course, the advice here also applies to the poetry in Paper 2.

Some people find it helps to subvocalise. This means you read the passage aloud to yourself in your head slowly – rather than reading it fast as if it were a story you were reading casually for fun at home. Others prefer to skim-read it once and then read it a second time, more slowly. Most people find it useful to read the passage more than once. Decide which method works best for you.

Read the sentence at the top of the page which introduces the passage and be sure to refer to any notes at the bottom of the passage which explain the meanings of more difficult words.

Read the questions

Read all the questions you are asked to answer, at least twice. Think about what they mean and make notes if you wish.

Never begin to write your answers before you have read both the passage and the questions thoroughly. You might like to highlight key words in the questions and the text as you read.

 Exam tip

The whole reading process can take several minutes. Do not panic if the person next to you begins writing immediately. Your answers will probably be better than his or hers because you have read and thought carefully before writing them.

Use the right style in your answers

Answer most questions in full sentences. It is usually incorrect to begin a sentence with 'because' or words like 'plus'.

Use a capital letter at the beginning and a full stop at the end of each whole sentence. If your answer needs other punctuation such as commas, then be careful where you place them.

If you are asked for short details or points from a passage (for example, you are asked to give another word for one that is in the passage to show that you understand it), then you need not use a whole sentence.

 Exam tip

Avoid slang and sloppy expressions such as 'like' (unless you mean similar to), 'cool' (unless you mean at a low-ish temperature) and *never* write 'and stuff'.

Stick closely to the information given in the passage in your answers but use your own words as much as you can.

Take great care with spelling. It is particularly careless to misspell a word which is in the passage or questions.

Be as precise as you can.

Answer as fully as you can

Put as much detail into your answers as you can. A good answer may need several sentences.

Highlight key words

If you are asked to summarise information from the passage, highlight the key words in the passage.

Then sum up whatever points you are asked about in your own words, quoting short phrases to make sure that your answer stays close to the passage. Do not put these phrases on separate lines. Weave them into your sentences and put inverted commas around them.

Don't forget that the purpose of all this is for you to show that you have understood the passage.

Use evidence from the passage

You must be able to prove, or back up, every answer with evidence from the passage. This is important, so:

- refer in your own words to what the writer says

- quote single words and short phrases (with inverted commas around them) woven into your answers

- look for, and comment on, parts of the passage in which the writer hints at something, but perhaps doesn't, for some reason, say it straightforwardly. In other words, ask yourself what lies under or behind the writer's words. You may have been taught to call this the 'subtext'.

 Exam tip

Think like a scientist. Look in the passage for evidence to 'prove' what you write.

2.2 Different types of writing

The passages(s) you are set to read can be fiction or non-fiction and will be one of the following:

- part of a novel or short story (look for characters, dialogue, imaginative description and sometimes a storyteller who is part of the story)

- part of a real-life story – a biography or autobiography (watch for the writer looking back at, or describing, personal events which happened in the past)

- a passage taken from a travel book – an account of the writer's experiences at a place he or she has visited or lived in (be prepared to write about the writer's thoughts and feelings about the place and his or her use of language)

- an extract from a play (be aware of what you learn about the characters from what they say and do and notice how the playwright uses stage directions).

2.3 Sample questions and answers

Try these yourself, covering up the sample answer. Then, when you've written your own response, compare it with the one given here.

Remember, though, that there are very few absolutely right or absolutely wrong answers in English. The answers given here are just suggestions as to how you might respond. The important thing is for you to be able to back up your answer with evidence from the passage.

Sample 1 (autobiography)

Look at the following sentence about South American screamer birds.

All we knew was that screamers were supposed to be entirely vegetarian, but whenever a butterfly hovered within six feet of Egbert, his whole being seemed to be filled with blood-lust, his eyes would take on a fanatical and most un-vegetarian-like gleam and he would endeavour to stalk it.

(From *The Drunken Forest* by Gerald Durrell, 1956)

Level 1 question

What do you learn about screamer birds from this sentence? (2)

Answer

They are vegetarian, but Egbert seems to want to eat butterflies.

Level 2 question

What amuses the writer about screamer birds? (2)

Answer

Although screamer birds are plant eaters, this particular one ('Egbert') seems strangely interested in watching and trying to catch butterflies. The writer is intrigued because such determination and the intent look in the bird's eyes humorously suggest that it is hard to believe it does not regard the butterfly as prey.

➔ Exam tip

Look at the number of marks given after each question on the exam paper. This is a guide as to how much you should write in your answers.

Sample 2 (fiction)

The narrator is walking through a wood towards a mysterious house.

Darkness swallowed me; the branches arched high overhead; I saw only glimpses of the paler sky through their tracery. My feet crunched beech mast. I smelled the coolness of the mossy earth and heard the trickle of water close by. As my eyes accustomed themselves to dimmer light, I saw that here, on the lower ground, a faint mist hung in the air, trapped perhaps beneath the trees. I must be careful not to stray from the path, which I could only dimly discern; but before many minutes had passed, wrought iron gates reared ahead of me, set in a wall of flint. Though I had reached the edge of the wood my way was barred. The gate must, however, be unlocked, as my arrival was expected.

(From *Set in Stone* by Linda Newbery, 2006)

Level 1 question

Sum up the narrator's thoughts and impressions as he approaches the gates. (4)

Answer

The narrator is uneasy as he can't see a lot through the mist. This makes him scared of losing the way. He feels slightly trapped by the trees and the fence, but he tries to convince himself everything will be all right as he is expected.

Level 2 question

How does the writer create a sense of anticipation as the narrator approaches the gates? (4)

Answer

The writer writes very sensually. All the narrator's senses are aroused by the dark, mysterious wood he is passing through at dusk on his way to gates leading to a property where he is an expected visitor. He hears 'crunched beech mast' under his feet and the sound of water nearby. He smells 'mossy earth' and can see trees, mist and, eventually, the big, rather sinister ('reared') gates in front of him. The writer evokes fear of the unfamiliar and a sense of unease by using short, quite jerky statements linked by semi-colons in the first sentence.

> In fiction, look at both what the characters say and at what the narrator says.

Sample 3 (fiction)

Jody follows the trail of his dying pony and finds buzzards with its body.

Jody leaped forward and plunged down the hill. The wet ground muffled his steps and the brush hid him. When he arrived it was all over. The first buzzard sat on the pony's head. Jody plunged into the circle like a cat. The black brotherhood rose in a cloud, but the big one on the pony's head was too late. As it hopped along to take off, Jody caught its wing tip and pulled it down. It was nearly as big as he was. The free wing crashed into his face with the force of a club but he hung on. The claws fastened on his leg and the wing elbows battered his head on either side. Jody groped wildly with his free hand; his fingers found the neck of the struggling bird. The red eyes looked into his face, calm and fearless and fierce: he held the bird's neck to the ground with one hand while with the other he found a piece of sharp white quartz. He struck again and again until the buzzard lay dead. He was still beating the dead bird when Billy Buck pulled him off and held him to calm his shaking.

(Slightly abridged from *The Red Pony* by John Steinbeck, 1937)

Level 1 question

Why does Jody kill the buzzard? (4)

Answer

Jody kills the buzzard 'on the pony's head' as he feels in some way the buzzards are responsible for the pony's death. He wants to take revenge for the death of his pony and grabs the first thing he feels has something to do with the death of his pony.

He is angry with the buzzards for eating his pony: 'He struck again and again'. The fact that he hits again and again shows he is letting go of his control and feelings and hitting the bird in his anger until it is more than dead.

Level 2 question

What can you deduce about Jody's reasons for killing the buzzard? (6)

Answer

Jody is beside himself with rage and distress because his pony has died and because, although he 'leaped' and 'plunged' in his hurry, he is too late to see the animal's last moments. Buzzards feed on freshly dead flesh and a group – looking sinister and greedy ('black brotherhood') – has been waiting near the dying, now dead, pony. Although he is quite young – the bird is not much smaller than he is – Jody launches a frenzied attack on the bird which has already perched on the pony's head ready to feed. He is not thinking rationally. The writer tells us that Jody 'groped wildly' and then he goes on hitting the bird with a piece of rock even after it is dead. He is probably full of adrenaline and extra strength because he is so upset and angry about his pony's death. He manages to hold onto the big bird despite its struggling and kills it even though it claws his leg and tries to beat him off with its strong wings. This is presented as the action of a boy who is frustrated and angry and wanting – or needing – to take his feelings out on something. Although if he lives in the country, he must know that the buzzards don't kill ponies.

> A full answer will make good use of evidence from the passage.

Sample 4 (drama)

Buddy's father Terry has broken the law but now wants an honest job.

Buddy Dad...

Terry You do two things. Buddy Clark: cry or say you're sorry, and you're out that door. Right?
(Buddy struggles not to cry but as his face screws up, Terry cuts in)

Terry I didn't 'ear you say 'Yes'.

Buddy Yes.

Terry And there's another fing before your mum starts in about where you bin. It might be six months before me trial comes up in court and I've promised 'er I'll get a job. You said them black friends – they still looking for drivers?
(Buddy runs to Terry and crushes himself against his chest. Carol closes the front door)

(From the TV script of *Buddy* by Nigel Hinton, 1987)

Level 1 question

Describe the relationship between Terry and Buddy in this extract. (4)

Answer

Buddy and Terry are son and father. Terry wants Buddy to be strong and manly as he tells him not to cry. But Terry is also strict as he demands that Buddy answer his question. Buddy cares a lot for Terry as he crushes himself to him to show he loves him and is pleased he is thinking of getting a job.

In drama, look closely at the stage directions as well as what the characters say.

Level 2 question

How does the playwright convey the relationship between Terry and Buddy in this extract? (5)

Answer

The playwright shows us Buddy, clearly distressed ('struggles not to cry') but having a reconciliation with his father Terry. The front door is open (Carol doesn't close it until the end of the passage) and we infer that Buddy has just arrived home after an unexplained absence because Terry tells Buddy that his mother will want to talk to him about where he's been. Both are trying to be brave. Terry has broken the law: 'It might be six months before me trial comes up.' In the meantime he is trying to reassure Buddy by telling him that he means to get an honest job. The playwright makes Terry speak with an accent and shows it in the script by spelling words such as 'fing' and 'bin' phonetically. It is probably an attempt by the playwright to make Terry sound natural and sincere as he makes his peace with Buddy. When Buddy hugs Terry wordlessly the playwright wants us to understand that they love and have forgiven each other. At the end of this passage the stage directions say that 'Carol closes the front door'. Dramatically this makes it clear that Buddy and Terry are together inside the house.

Sample 5 (travel writing)

The author describes his natural, open-air bath.

Near the house was one of the miracles of El Valero: a torrent of water that rushed out from a rock and tumbled into a little pool below. I sat in the pool and poured bucketful after bucketful over my head and body. There was a soapdish and a bottle of shampoo and towels and some washing hanging from a wire strung between two acacia trees. Without needing to put shoes or clothes on, I could take just five paces and pick oranges, mandarins, figs or grapes, fresh from the trees. I cooled them in the waterfall and stuffed myself.

(From *Driving Over Lemons* by Chris Stewart, 1999)

Level 1 question

Sum up in your own words what the writer likes about his outdoor shower. (3)

Answer

The writer likes that the shower is completely natural, calling it a 'miracle'. He can sit in the pool and pour bucketfuls of water over himself, which he also likes. Finally he likes that he can pick fruit from nearby trees after having had a shower.

As with fiction, in travel writing think about how the writer brings alive the place he or she is describing.

Level 2 question

Why does the writer regard his outdoor shower as 'one of the miracles of El Valero'? (4)

Answer

He is impressed and entranced because the waterfall – which is effectively an outdoor shower – is completely natural. The water gushes out of a rock into a pool which he can use as a bath. And someone has left soap, shampoo and towels for him so showering out of doors is clearly accepted practice at El Valero. The same person has apparently also hung out washing to dry and that adds to the novelty. The writer also marvels at being able to pick fruits from trees very close to the shower and eat them without dressing himself. We infer that it is hot. He is quite comfortable naked in the open air, has to cool his fruit before eating it and the washing is drying in the sunshine. The waterfall and pool provides respite from the heat and sun which adds to his enthusiastic enjoyment ('bucketful after bucketful') of it.

Sample 6 (autobiography)

As an adult, Frank McCourt recalls how, as children, he and his siblings would settle down for the night.

Soon we're all in bed and if there's the odd flea I don't mind because it's warm in the bed with the six of us and I love the glow of the fire – the way it dances on the walls and ceiling and makes the room go red and black, red and black, till it dims to white and black and all you can hear is a little cry from Oliver turning in my mother's arms.

(From *Angela's Ashes* by Frank McCourt, 1996)

Level 1 question

How does the writer feel about going to bed? (3)

Answer

He likes going to bed as it is warm, and because of that he doesn't mind the fleas. He also likes the fire and watching its light on the wall and ceiling.

As with all writing, when you read biography or autobiography look closely at details the writer has included and think about what they add.

Level 2 question

What techniques does the writer use to make this description of the children's bedtime vivid? (3)

Answer

Although he is looking back as an adult, the writer uses the present tense rather than the past to create a sense that the reader is inside the mind of the child. He writes sensually – telling us how it feels to be in the bed (warm), what he can see (reflections of the fire on the ceiling) and hear (Oliver crying). He uses repetition to suggest the soporific flickering of the fire flames as the room grows quiet and the six family members (presumably) fall asleep.

2.4 Practice tasks

Now practise your skills on these tasks which are examples of what you can expect in Paper 1 Section A.

The marks at the end of each question are a guide as to how much you should write in your answers.

You should spend around 35 minutes in total on each task. Spend the first 5 minutes planning. Write for about 25 minutes. Read your work through in the last 5 minutes to check for mistakes and to make small changes.

There are suggestions to show you how to write good answers in the Answer guidance section, pages 72–82. Do not look at these until you've tried each exercise yourself. Then consult the suggestions to see how you might have done it better.

1 Fiction

Level 1

A sudden disaster has struck London. Nearly all its population has been blinded. The narrator is one of the few who can still see.

I crossed in the direction of Piccadilly. I was about to start along it when I noticed a steady tapping not far away, and coming closer. A man, more neatly dressed than any other I had seen that morning, was walking rapidly towards me, hitting the wall beside him with a white stick. As he caught the sound of
5   my steps he stopped, listening alertly.

'It's all right,' I told him. 'Come on.'

I felt relieved to see him. He was, so to speak, normally blind. His dark glasses were much less disturbing than the staring but useless eyes of others.

'Stand still, then,' he said. 'I've already been bumped into by God knows
10 how many fools today. Why is it so quiet? I know it isn't night – I can feel the sunlight. What's gone wrong with everything?'

I told him as much as I knew.

He said nothing for almost a minute. Then he gave a short, bitter laugh.

'There's one thing,' he said. 'They'll be needing all their damned patronage for
15 themselves now.' With that he straightened up, a little defiantly.

'Thank you. Good luck,' he said to me, and set off westwards wearing an exaggerated air of independence.

The sound of his briskly confident tapping gradually died away behind me as I made my way up Piccadilly.
20   There were no people to be seen now, and I walked among the scatter of stranded vehicles in the road. Out there I was much less disturbing to the people feeling their way along the fronts of the buildings, for every time they heard a step close by they would stop and brace themselves against a possible collision. Such collisions were taking place all down the street, but there was
25 one I found significant. The subjects of it had been groping along a shop front from opposite directions when they met with a bump. One was a young man wearing a well-cut suit, but wearing a tie obviously selected by touch alone: the other a woman who carried a small child. [...]

'Wait a minute,' he said. 'Can your child see?'
30   'Yes,' she said. 'But I can't.'

The young man turned. He put one finger on the plate-glass window, pointing.

'Look, Sonny, what's in there?' he asked.

'Not Sonny,' the child objected.

'Go on, Mary. Tell the gentleman,' her mother encouraged her.
35   'Pretty ladies,' said the child.

The man took the woman by the arm, and felt his way to the next window.

'And what's in here?' he asked again.

'Apples and fings,' the child told him.

'Fine!' said the young man.

40 He pulled off his shoe, and hit the window with a smart smack with the heel of it. The crash reverberated up and down the street. He restored his shoe, put an arm cautiously through the broken window, and felt about until he found a couple of oranges. One he gave to the woman and one to the child. He felt about again, found one for himself, and began to peel it. The woman fingered hers.

45 'But –' she began.

'What's the matter? Don't like oranges?' he asked.

'This isn't right,' she said 'We didn't ought to take 'em. Not like this.'

'How else are you going to get food?' he inquired.

(Slightly abridged from *The Day of the Triffids* by John Wyndham, 1951)

1 Look carefully at paragraph 1. Why is the writer surprised? (1)

2 Choose three words or phrases from lines 1–17 which show what impresses the narrator about the man with the white stick. (3)

Explain your choices. (6)

3 What does the writer want us to know about the young man in the suit in lines 26–48? (4)

4 What do we learn about the woman in lines 28–48? (4)

5 Write one short quotation from any part of the passage which shows how quiet London now is. (1)

Explain your choice. (2)

6 The woman does not want to steal. How does the writer make this clear? (4)

Explain your views. (4)

Level 2

A sudden disaster has struck London. Nearly all its population has been blinded. The narrator is one of the few who can still see.

Still magnetically drawn towards the old centre of things, I crossed in the direction of Piccadilly.

I was about to start along it when I noticed a sharp new sound – a steady tapping not far away, and coming closer. Looking up I discovered its source. A

5 man, more neatly dressed than any other I had seen that morning, was walking rapidly towards me, hitting the wall beside him with a white stick. As he caught the sound of my steps he stopped, listening alertly.

'It's all right,' I told him. 'Come on.'

I felt relieved to see him. He was, so to speak, normally blind. His dark glasses

10 were much less disturbing than the staring but useless eyes of others.

'Stand still, then,' he said. 'I've already been bumped into by God knows how many fools today. What the devil's happened? Why is it so quiet? I know it isn't night – I can feel the sunlight. What's gone wrong with everything?'

I told him as much as I knew.

15 When I had finished he said nothing for almost a minute, then he gave a short, bitter laugh. 'There's one thing,' he said. 'They'll be needing all their damned patronage for themselves now.'

With that he straightened up, a little defiantly.

'Thank you. Good luck,' he said to me, and set off westwards wearing an

20 exaggerated air of independence.

The sound of his briskly confident tapping gradually died away behind me as I made my way up Piccadilly.

There were no people to be seen now, and I walked among the scatter of stranded vehicles in the road. Out there I was much less disturbing to the people

25 feeling their way along the fronts of the buildings, for every time they heard a step close by they would stop and brace themselves against a possible collision. Such collisions were taking place every now and then all down the street, but there was one I found significant. The subjects of it had been groping along a shop front from opposite directions when they met with a bump. One was
30 a young man wearing a well-cut suit, but wearing a tie obviously selected by touch alone: the other a woman who carried a small child. The child whined something inaudible. The young man had started to edge his way past the woman. He stopped abruptly.

'Wait a minute,' he said. 'Can your child see?'
35 'Yes,' she said. 'But I can't.'

The young man turned. He put one finger on the plate-glass window, pointing.

'Look, Sonny, what's in there?' he asked.

'Not Sonny,' the child objected.
40 'Go on, Mary. Tell the gentleman,' her mother encouraged her.

'Pretty ladies,' said the child.

The man took the woman by the arm, and felt his way to the next window.

'And what's in here?' he asked again. 'Apples and fings,' the child told him.

'Fine!' said the young man.
45 He pulled off his shoe, and hit the window with a smart smack with the heel of it. He was inexperienced: the first blow did not do it, but the second did. The crash reverberated up and down the street. He restored his shoe, put an arm cautiously through the broken window, and felt about until he found a couple of oranges. One he gave to the woman and one to the child. He
50 felt about again, found one for himself, and began to peel it. The woman fingered hers.

'But –' she began.

'What's the matter? Don't like oranges?' he asked.

'This isn't right,' she said. 'We didn't ought to take 'em. Not like this.'
55 'How else are you going to get food?' he inquired.

(From *The Day of the Triffids* by John Wyndham, 1951)

1	What atmosphere is created in the first paragraph?	(3)
2	How does the writer stress the horror of sudden blindness?	(4)
3	What qualities does the writer give to the man with the white stick?	(6)
4	What effect is created by the introduction of the woman with the child?	(6)
5	How does the writer use dialogue and other techniques to shape our response to the horror of the situation in the passage?	(6)

2 Travel writing

Level 1

Frances Mayes, an American university teacher, and her husband Ed, have bought a house in Tuscany in Italy but it is not yet as they would like it to be.

I admire the beauty of scorpions. They look like black-ink hieroglyphs of themselves. I'm fascinated, too, that they can navigate by the stars, though how they ever glimpse constellations from their usual homes in dusty corners of vacant houses, I don't know. One scurries around in the bidet every morning.
5 Several get sucked into the new vacuum cleaner by mistake, though usually they are luckier: I trap them in a jar and take them outside. I suspect every cup and shoe. When I fluff a bed pillow, an albino one lands on my bare shoulder. [...] Other than these inhabitants, the inheritance from the former occupants consists of dusty wine bottles – thousands and thousands in the shed and in the stalls. We
10 fill local recycling bins over and over, waterfalls of glass raining from the boxes we've loaded and reloaded. [Outhouses] are piled with rusted pans, newspapers

from 1958, wire, paint cans, debris. Whole eco-systems of spiders and scorpions are destroyed, though hours later they seem to have regenerated. I look for old photos or antique spoons but see nothing of interest except some handmade iron
15 tools. [...] One cunningly made tool, an elegant little sculpture, is a hand-sized crescent with a worn chestnut handle. Any Tuscan would recognize it in a second: a tool for trimming grapes.

When we first saw the house, it was filled with fanciful iron beds with painted medallions of Mary and shepherds holding lambs, wormy chests of drawers with
20 marble tops, cribs, foxed mirrors, cradles, boxes, and lugubrious bleeding-heart religious pictures of the Crucifixion. The owner removed everything [...] except a thirties kitchen cupboard and an ugly red bed that we cannot figure out how to get down the narrow back stairs from the third floor. Finally we take the bed apart and throw it piece by piece from the window.

25 Local people, out for afternoon strolls, pause in the road and look up at all the mad activity, the car trunk full of bottles, mattress flying, me screaming as a scorpion falls down my shirt when I sweep the stone walls of the stall, Ed wielding a grim-reaper scythe through the weeds. Sometimes they stop and call up 'How much did you pay for the house?'

30 I'm taken aback and charmed by the bluntness. 'Probably too much,' I answer. One person remembered that long ago an artist from Naples lived there; for most it has stood empty as far back as they can remember.

Every day we haul and scrub. We are becoming as parched as the hills around us. We have bought cleaning supplies, a new stove and fridge. With sawhorses
35 and two planks we set up a kitchen counter. Although we must bring hot water from the bathroom in a plastic laundry pan, we have a surprisingly manageable kitchen. As one who has used **Williams-Sonoma** as a toy store for years, I begin to get an elementary sense of the kitchen. Three wooden spoons, two for the salad, one for stirring. A sauté pan, bread knife, cutting knife, cheese grater,
40 pasta pot, baking dish and stove-top espresso pot. We brought over some old picnic silverware and bought a few glasses and plates.

Those first pastas are divine. After long work, we eat everything in sight then tumble like field hands into bed.

(Abridged from *Under the Tuscan Sun* by Frances Mayes, 1996)

Note: Williams-Sonoma is an American shop that sells elaborate kitchenware.

1   Look carefully at paragraph 1.

What does the writer like about:

a) scorpions?   (2)

b) the tools she finds?   (2)

2   Choose two words or phrases from paragraph 1 which show how the writer feels about nature.   (2)

Explain your choices.   (4)

3   Why do you think the writer tells us what local people have said?   (4)

4   Write two quotations which say something vivid or interesting about the house, its contents or surroundings.   (2)

Explain what your quotations suggest about the place the writer is describing.   (4)

5   The writer and her husband are changing as they work on the house. Explain how you know this from the last two paragraphs.   (5)

Level 2

Frances Mayes, an American university teacher, and her husband Ed, have bought a house in Tuscany in Italy but it is not yet as they would like it to be.

I admire the beauty of scorpions. They look like black-ink hieroglyphs of themselves. I'm fascinated, too, that they can navigate by the stars, though how they ever glimpse constellations from their usual homes in dusty corners of vacant houses, I don't know. One scurries around in the bidet every morning. Several get

5　sucked into the new vacuum cleaner by mistake, though usually they are luckier: I trap them in a jar and take them outside. I suspect every cup and shoe. When I fluff a bed pillow, an albino one lands on my bare shoulder. We upset armies of spiders as we empty the closet under the stairs of its bottle collection. Impressive, the long threads for legs and the fly-sized bodies; I can even see their eyes. Other

10　than these inhabitants, the inheritance from the former occupants consists of dusty wine bottles – thousands and thousands in the shed and in the stalls. We fill local recycling bins over and over, waterfalls of glass raining from the boxes we've loaded and reloaded. The stalls and limonaia (a garage-sized room on the side of the house once used for storing lemons during the winter) are piled with

15　rusted pans, newspapers from 1958, wire, paint cans, debris. Whole eco-systems of spiders and scorpions are destroyed, though hours later they seem to have regenerated. I look for old photos or antique spoons but see nothing of interest except some handmade iron tools and a 'priest', a swan-shaped wooden form with a hook for a hanging pan of hot coals, which was pushed under bedcovers

20　in winter to warm the clammy sheets. One cunningly made tool, an elegant little sculpture, is a hand-sized crescent with a worn chestnut handle. Any Tuscan would recognize it in a second: a tool for trimming grapes.

When we first saw the house, it was filled with fanciful iron beds with painted medallions of Mary and shepherds holding lambs, wormy chests of drawers with

25　marble tops, cribs, foxed mirrors, cradles, boxes, and lugubrious bleeding-heart religious pictures of the Crucifixion. The owner removed everything – down to the switchplate covers and lightbulbs – except a thirties kitchen cupboard and an ugly red bed that we cannot figure out how to get down the narrow back stairs from the third floor. Finally we take the bed apart and throw it piece by piece from the window.

30　The Cortonese, out for afternoon strolls, pause in the road and look up at all the mad activity, the car trunk full of bottles, mattress flying, me screaming as a scorpion falls down my shirt when I sweep the stone walls of the stall, Ed wielding a grim-reaper scythe through the weeds. Sometimes they stop and call up 'How much did you pay for the house?'

35　I'm taken aback and charmed by the bluntness. 'Probably too much,' I answer. One person remembered that long ago an artist from Naples lived there; for most it has stood empty as far back as they can remember.

Every day we haul and scrub. We are becoming as parched as the hills around us. We have bought cleaning supplies, a new stove and fridge. With sawhorses

40　and two planks we set up a kitchen counter. Although we must bring hot water from the bathroom in a plastic laundry pan, we have a surprisingly manageable kitchen. As one who has used **Williams-Sonoma** as a toy store for years, I begin to get an elementary sense of the kitchen. Three wooden spoons, two for the salad, one for stirring. A sauté pan, bread knife, cutting knife, cheese grater,

45　pasta pot, baking dish and stove-top espresso pot. We brought over some old picnic silverware and bought a few glasses and plates.

Those first pastas are divine. After long work, we eat everything in sight then tumble like field hands into bed.

(From *Under the Tuscan Sun* by Frances Mayes, 1996)

Note: Williams-Sonoma is an American shop that sells elaborate kitchenware.

1　What does the writer find fascinating about scorpions? (2)

2　What interests her about the tools she finds? (2)

3　What do you learn about the writer's attitude to nature from the first paragraph? Use quotations from the passage to illustrate your views. (4)

4   What effect is created by the conversations with local people?   (4)

5   How is contrast used in this passage to create a sense of place?   (6)

6   How does the writer suggest, in the last two paragraphs, that as they work
     on the house, she and Ed are changing?   (7)

3 Biography/Autobiographical writing

Level 1

Actress Meera Syal grew up in the West Midlands, the daughter of parents who had come to England from India in the 1970s to make a better life for themselves and their children. This is a semi-autobiographical work, with 'Meena' as the fictional narrator.

My mother knew from experience that she would get fewer stares and whispers if she had donned any of the sensible teacher's trouser suits she would wear for school, but for her, looking glamorous in saris and formal Indian suits was part of the English people's education. It was her duty to show them that we could wear discreet
5   gold jewellery, dress in tasteful silks and speak English without an accent.

During our very special shopping outings to Birmingham, she would often pass other Indian women in the street and they would stare at each other in that innocent, direct way of two rare species who have just found out they are vaguely related. These other Indian women would inevitably be dressed in embroidered shalwar kameez
10 suits screaming with green and pinks and yellows (incongruous with thick woolly socks squeezed into open-toed sandals and men's cardies over their vibrating thin silks, evil necessities in this damn cold country) with bright make-up and showy gold-plated jewellery which made them look like ambulating Christmas trees.

Mama would acknowledge them with a respectful nod and then turn away
15 and shake her head. 'In the village, they would look beautiful. But not here. There is no sun to light them up. Under clouds, they look like they are dressed for a discotheque.'

But she was quiet now, no light in her face. Papa said, 'Have something to eat. A cake. Have one of those ... what you like ... those meringue things.'
20 'She won't,' I chipped in, scraping my fork into the spongy belly of my rum baba. 'You know what she will say, I can make this cheaper at home.' [...]

'That's enough!' barked Papa. 'Mind your manners now or we're going home!'

My mother shook her head at him and put her hand over mine. I snatched it away and finished my cake in silence.
25 My father showed he was sorry by buying me a hot dog on the way home. I sat in the back of the Mini and concentrated on licking the tomato sauce off my fingertips whilst singing 'Bobbing Along on the Bottom of the Beautiful Briny Sea' in between slurps.

Mummy and Papa were talking again, soft whispers, sssssssss, my mother's
30 bracelets jingled as she seemed to wipe something from her face. This was my birthday and they were leaving me out again. I squeezed my hot dog and suddenly the sausage shot into my mouth and lodged into my windpipe. I was too shocked to move, my fingers curled uselessly into my fists. They were still talking, engrossed, I could see Papa's eyes in the mirror, darting from my mother's face to
35 the unfolding road. I thought of writing SAUSAGE STUCK on the windscreen and then realised I could not spell sausage. I was going to die in the back of the car and somewhere inside me, I felt thrilled. It was so dramatic. This was by far the most exciting thing that had ever happened to me.

(Abridged from *Anita and Me* by Meera Syal, 1996)

1   Look at paragraph 1.

How does the narrator's mother like to dress?   (2)

Why does she dress in this way?   (2)

2 Look at paragraphs 1 and 2. How well (or not) does the narrator get on with her mother? (4)

3 From the whole passage how well (or not) do the narrator's parents get on with each other? Refer to a) how they speak to each other, b) how they speak to the writer and c) how they behave. (5)

4 Look at the final paragraph. What do you find amusing here?

You might choose to write about: the stuck sausage, the parents' not noticing, the way the narrator exaggerates. (6)

5 What do you learn about the narrator from this passage?

You could include her attitude to her parents, her love of food, her use of language. (6)

Level 2

Actress Meera Syal grew up in the West Midlands, the daughter of parents who had come to England from India in the 1970s to make a better life for themselves and their children. This is a semi-autobiographical work, with 'Meena' as the fictional narrator.

My mother knew from experience that she would get fewer stares and whispers if she had donned any of the sensible teacher's trouser suits she would wear for school, but for her, looking glamorous in saris and formal Indian suits was part of the English people's education. It was her duty to show them that we could wear discreet
5 gold jewellery, dress in tasteful silks and speak English without an accent.

During our very special shopping outings to Birmingham, she would often pass other Indian women in the street and they would stare at each other in that innocent, direct way of two rare species who have just found out they are vaguely related. These other Indian women would inevitably be dressed in embroidered
10 shalwar kameez suits screaming with green and pinks and yellows (incongruous with thick woolly socks squeezed into open-toed sandals and men's cardies over their vibrating thin silks, evil necessities in this damn cold country) with bright make-up and showy gold-plated jewellery which made them look like ambulating Christmas trees.
15 Mama would acknowledge them with a respectful nod and then turn away and shake her head. 'In the village, they would look beautiful. But not here. There is no sun to light them up. Under clouds, they look like they are dressed for a discotheque.'

But she was quiet now, no light in her face. Papa said, 'Have something to eat.
20 A cake. Have one of those ... what you like ... those meringue things.'

'She won't,' I chipped in, scraping my fork into the spongy belly of my rum baba. 'You know what she will say, I can make this cheaper at home.' My mother never ate out, never, always affronted by paying for some over-boiled, under-seasoned dish of slop when she knew she could rustle up a hot, heartwarming
25 meal from a few leftover vegetables and a handful of spices. 'I bet you couldn't make this at home,' I continued. 'How would you make a cake? How would you get it round and get the cream to stand up and the cherry to balance like this? You have to buy some things, you can't do everything you know ...?'

'That's enough!' barked Papa. 'Mind your manners now or we're going home!'
30 My mother shook her head at him and put her hand over mine. I snatched it away and finished my cake in silence.

My father showed he was sorry by buying me a hot dog on the way home. I sat in the back of the Mini and concentrated on licking the tomato sauce off my fingertips whilst singing 'Bobbing Along on the Bottom of the Beautiful Briny
35 Sea' in between slurps.

Mummy and Papa were talking again, soft whispers, sssssssss, my mother's bracelets jingled as she seemed to wipe something from her face. This was

my birthday and they were leaving me out again. I squeezed my hot dog and
40   suddenly the sausage shot into my mouth and lodged into my windpipe. I was too
shocked to move, my fingers curled uselessly into my fists. They were still talking,
engrossed, I could see Papa's eyes in the mirror, darting from my mother's face to
the unfolding road. I thought of writing SAUSAGE STUCK on the windscreen
and then realised I could not spell sausage. I was going to die in the back of the car
45   and somewhere inside me, I felt thrilled. It was so dramatic. This was by far the
most exciting thing that had ever happened to me.

(From *Anita and Me* by Meera Syal, 1996)

1   What does paragraph 1 tell us:

    a) about the narrator's mother and her attitudes?   (2)

    b) the narrator's own feelings about her mother's views?   (2)

2   How does the narrator indicate the tension between her mother and
herself in paragraph 5? Use quotations from the passage to illustrate your
explanation.   (4)

3   What does this passage reveal about the relationship between her parents
as observed and remembered by the narrator?   (5)

4   How does the narrator make the final paragraph funny?   (6)

5   What impression is the narrator trying to create of herself in this passage?   (6)

4 Drama

Joey and Topthorn are horses that are being trained to work in the war zones
of France in the First World War. In the play the horses are represented by very
impressive life-size puppets, each operated by three visible puppeteers.

Military Stables, 6 November 1914
Nicholls   *(to Joey)* Training's nearly over but you're not ready for war yet.
Nicholls suddenly fires a round from a pistol near Joey's head. Joey reacts.
Nicholls is intending to 'desensitise' Joey – making him used to it.
        Good boy. This is a gun. The smell is cordite. Try again.
Fires another round. Joey reacts.
        Good boy.
Fires another. Joey reacts.
        Good boy, Joey.
Enter Captain Stewart.
Nicholls fires two or three rapid rounds.
        Good boy. You'll get used to it ... Imagine if these creatures
        suddenly evolved – that they became as warlike and violent
        as us.
Stewart   That's an odd thought.
Nicholls   You think I'm odd?
Stewart   Oh, no, I didn't mean that, I mean I've never thought that
        about horses.
Nicholls   I hadn't until just then. *(Calls)* Trooper Warren?
Ned   Sir!
Nicholls   *(to Stewart)* We're posted to France in the morning.
Stewart   In the morning it is.
Nicholls   Tell the men to stop polishing.
Ned   What, zur?!
Nicholls   Battle orders; no polishing – buttons, cap badges, buckles,
        stirrup irons – let them all go dull. We don't want anything
        to flash in the sun and give us away – I know, Warren, after
        all that hard work.
Ned   Sir.
Exit Ned.

Nicholls	How's your troop?
Stewart	Ready for battle, sir.
Nicholls	I was pleased with the practice charge today. Were you and Topthorn far behind?
Stewart	We were breathing right down your neck, as you well know. I wouldn't like to be on the wrong end of our charge. My uncle says men tend to go to pieces when our cavalry bear down on them. He's seen men flee or press themselves into the ground. And even if they keep their positions, there weren't many who could face our cavalry and keep their composure – to aim straight as it were. We're going to cut a swathe through **Fritz**, he won't know what's hit him. He'll wish that he'd never been born, he'll –
Nicholls	Well, we're about to discover if all that's true, aren't we? I'm not casting aspersions on your uncle's experience, but every generation has to discover things for themselves, don't they? There's some things that can be understood through telling, but other things have to be experienced before they can be fully apprehended. War is one such thing. How do Joey and Topthorn get on?
Stewart	They're a bit snippy, sir.
Nicholls	I wasn't imagining it, then. What's that about?
Stewart	Two proud animals, sir.
Nicholls	Is Topthorn out in the paddock?
Stewart	Yes.
Nicholls	I'll take Joey out to him. Tell the men to prepare, will you? **Reveille** at five thirty.

Exit Stewart.

The scene becomes a paddock.

Enter Topthorn. Joey and Topthorn react to one another.

> Joey, listen. Sort out who's in charge. No fighting – save all that for Fritz ... You'll be all right, won't you boys? I just hope that I'm up to it when the time comes. You think I'll be up to it?

Joey and Topthorn are only interested in each other. Exit Nicholls.

(From *War Horse*, play by Nick Stafford, 2007, based on the novel by Michael Morpurgo, 1982)

Note: Fritz is a British slang for a German.
Reveille is an army term for a wake-up call blown on a bugle.

Level 1

1   Look carefully at the first part of this scene.

   a) Why is Nicholls firing bullets near Joey? (1)

   b) How is Joey reacting? (1)

2   **a)** Why does Nicholls tell Ned to stop polishing equipment? (1)

   b) How do you know that Ned is not happy with Nicholls's order? (1)

3   Choose two words or phrases (from the spoken text or the stage directions) which tell you something interesting about Joey or Topthorn or both. (2)

   Explain your choices. (4)

4   Read carefully what Stewart says about fighting. Sum up how he feels about going into battle. (3)

5   There are three men in this scene. Write a sentence or two about each of them, naming them and explaining how different they are from each other. (6)

6   Write two quotations which show how tense everyone is in this scene. (2)

   Explain your choices fully. (4)

★ Make sure you know

- ★ That there are four different types of literary prose comprehension passage which you might be set in Paper 1: fiction, travel writing, (auto)biography and drama.

- ★ How to approach the literary prose comprehension passage in Paper 1.

- ★ The style of answer you should use when responding to each type of question.

3 Poetry comprehension

In Paper 2 Section A you will be given a poem or part of a poem to read. You will then be asked to answer questions or to write about the poem to show how well you have understood and responded to it.

The same poem or extract will be set at both levels. As with the literary prose comprehension the questions and tasks will be set out in more detail at Level 1.

The poetry question is your chance to show that you:

- are aware of how language is used in poetry

- can write what you think based on your reading of the poem

- understand how poets show the reader what they are feeling or thinking

- have learnt about metaphor, simile, personification, symbols, irony, alliteration, assonance, rhyme, rhythm and metre and how they can be used to create different effects.

You should answer the questions using full sentences, unless indicated otherwise.

If you really don't know the answer, make a sensible guess by looking for clues in the poem, and give your reasons.

Spend time thinking and making notes before writing your answers.

If you are asked to use your imagination to continue the theme of a poem, remember that this is still a question to see if you have understood the poem. So the more you base your imaginative answer on what is in the poem, the more marks you will get.

3.1 Poetic techniques

Before you can tackle a poetry comprehension you need an understanding of the techniques poets use to achieve their effects. Think of these as a poet's 'tools' if it helps. The examiners expect you to be familiar with ten key techniques.

> Remember that good prose writing will use these techniques too.

Metaphor

A metaphor is the comparison of one thing with another by pretending that the thing described really is what it is being compared with.

Metaphors are not literally true. Like personification or a simile, a metaphor is a form of image. The adjective 'metaphorical' and the adverb 'metaphorically' are useful terms to include in your writing too.

> **Examples**
>
> *The wind was a torrent of darkness*
>
> *When the road is a ribbon of moonlight*
>
> (Both from 'The Highwayman' by Alfred Noyes)

Simile

A simile is a comparison of one thing with another which makes it clear that it is a comparison by using the word 'like' or 'as'. It is another sort of image.

Examples

the Land / Was sodden as the bed of an ancient lake

Rain plastered the land till it was shining / Like hammered lead

(Both from 'November' by Ted Hughes)

Personification

Personification is the giving of human qualities and abilities to non-humans. Poets often personify things as a way of describing them. Personification creates an image or picture in the reader's mind.

Examples

The winds were lovesick with her

(From *Antony and Cleopatra* by William Shakespeare)

the moon walked the night

(From 'Silver' by Walter de la Mare)

Symbol

A symbol is an object which stands for something else, as a badge or emblem does. A national flag is a symbol of a country.

Examples

In 'The Rime of the Ancient Mariner' by Samuel Taylor Coleridge the narrator shoots an albatross and has to wear it round his neck as a punishment. The wearing of the albatross is a symbol of sin.

A rose by any other name would smell as sweet

(From *Romeo and Juliet* by William Shakespeare)

The rose is a symbol of Juliet's passionate love for Romeo.

The merry bells ring

To welcome the spring

(From 'The Echoing Green' by William Blake)

The bells are a symbol of the change which comes with spring.

Irony

Irony is a figure of speech in which what is said is the opposite of what is meant. It is often 'dry' and funny.

Examples

Within the human world I know

Such goings on could not be so,

For human beings only do

What their religion tells them to.

(From 'Diary of a Church Mouse' by John Betjeman)

The poet really means that most people are hypocrites who do exactly the opposite of what their religion tells them to.

Alliteration

Alliteration is the repetition of a consonant sound at the beginning of words that are close to each other. You can also use the adjective 'alliterative'.

Example

downward smoke, the slender stream

(From 'The Lotus-Eaters' by Alfred Lord Tennyson)

And through his britches the blue winds blow

(From 'Timothy Winters' by Charles Causley)

Assonance

Assonance is the repetition of the same vowel sound (not necessarily spelt the same way) inside neighbouring words. You can also use the adjective 'assonant'.

Examples

plump, unpecked cherries

(From 'Goblin Market' by Christina Rossetti)

I've lice in my tunic and a cold in my nose

(From 'Roman Wall Blues' by W.H. Auden)

Rhyme

Rhyme is the patterns made by the ends of words which sound the same or similar. There are several sorts of rhyme.

Examples

The Miller was a chap of sixteen stone.

A great stout fellow big in brawn and bone

(From *The Canterbury Tales* by Geoffrey Chaucer, translated by Nevil Coghill)

These lines from *The Canterbury Tales* have a full rhyme.

My last dear fuel of life to heap upon my soul

And kindle my will to a flame that shall consume

Their dross of indifference and take the toll

(From 'Last Lesson of the Afternoon' by D.H. Lawrence)

The first and third lines have a half rhyme – 'soul' and 'toll' almost, but don't quite, rhyme.

Where the wheat is sweet as an angel's feet

(From 'Cowboy Song' by Charles Causley)

This line has an internal rhyme. The rhyming words are within rather than at the end of the line.

Rhythm

Rhythm is the musical pattern of beats, stressed sounds, unstressed sounds and pauses which give a poem its shape. It can be regular or free.

Examples

Four o'clock strikes,

There's a rising hum,

Then the doors fly open.

The children come

(From 'Out of School' by Hal Summers)

The lines above have a regular rhythm with two strong beats in each line (beats underlined).

Glory be to God for dappled things

For skies of couple-colour as a brinded cow

(From 'Pied Beauty' by Gerard Manley Hopkins)

The lines have a much more regular rhythm, with every second syllable having a stress/beat.

Nobody heard him, the dead man,

But still he lay moaning

I was much further out than you thought

(From 'Not Waving but Drowning' by Stevie Smith)

The lines above have an irregular rhythm (once again the beats have been underlined).

Metre

Metre is the pattern of sound units in lines of verse. Just as music has bars, separated by bar lines, with up beats and down beats inside them, so lines of poetry are divided into feet. Feet are units of two or three syllables which are indicated by forward slashes.

If mu / sic be / the food / of love / play on

(From *Twelfth Night* by William Shakespeare)

Merrily / merrily / shall I live / now

(From *The Tempest* by William Shakespeare)

Bubble / bubble / toil and / trouble

(From *Macbeth* by William Shakespeare)

If you say these lines aloud in an exaggerated way you will hear that the rhythm in each of the three lines above is different because of where you have to put the stresses in the feet. For example we say BU-bble not bu-BBLE and MER-ri-ly not mer-ri-LY or mer-RI-ly and this placement of the stress affects the rhythm of our speech.

Using these terms in your writing

Although you need to be familiar with the ten terms above, be careful how you use them. Examiners will not give marks for what they call 'device spotting'. They expect you to use the terms to show how the poet is creating his or her effects.

> Use words such as 'effect' and expressions such as 'The poet asks/wonders/creates/ suggests' in your writing about poetry.

Imagine you are writing about these opening lines from G.K. Chesterton's 'The Donkey':

> *When fishes flew and forests walked*
>
> *And figs grew upon thorn*

You will get no marks for writing the following and then moving on to another point:

The poet uses alliteration in the first two lines.

You will, however, get marks for writing something like this:

The poet's use of alliteration in the first two lines helps to suggest a topsy-turvy ancient world in which nothing is as we know it now. The repeated 'f', a soft sound, makes it sound gentle, reassuring and convincing so that we are drawn into the story – a bit like 'Once upon a time' in a fairy story.

> Do not stop at identifying the poet's tools. Comment on the effects that he or she has created.

Here's another example based on the opening of John Keats's poem 'To Autumn'.

> *Season of mists and mellow fruitfulness,*
>
> *Close bosom-friend of the maturing sun*

Do not just write:

The second line is an example of personification.

Instead write something such as:

The poet personifies the declining sun to suggest that it is a relative of the season autumn (also personified because that's who the poem is addressed to). Together the two are responsible for the ripening of the autumn fruits and the mists as the season changes. By addressing first autumn and then the sun as if they were people Keats creates a sense that the onset of autumn is an intimate, 'hands on' process managed by forces with personalities.

> It is sometimes easier to comment on a poet's effects if you use adjectives related to the technique, such as 'assonant' or 'ironic' rather than the nouns 'assonance' and 'irony'. Verbs such as 'symbolises' or 'personifies' are useful too.

3.2 Approaching a poem

In your exam you will, almost certainly, be faced with a poem you have never seen before. The examiners want to see how well you can read, understand and respond to it in a fairly short time.

Make sure you spend enough time reading and thinking about the poem before you try to answer the questions.

Read it through quickly once. Then read it a second time more slowly – aloud to yourself in your head – so that you hear the rhyme, rhythm and metre as well as seeing it on the page. Poetry is very close to music. It needs to be heard as well as read if you're going to respond to it fully. Listen inside your head to the sound of the poem's words while you are in your exam.

When you are reading, look closely at the poem's punctuation to make sure you get the full sense of its meaning.

Remember that:

- sentences and phrases do not always finish at the ends of lines

- full stops, commas and other marks of punctuation are often placed in the middle of lines

- sometimes there is no punctuation at the ends of stanzas because sentences flow from one stanza to the next.

Read the poem a third time. Then tackle the questions.

3.3 Sample questions and answers

Try these yourself, covering up the sample answer. Then, when you've written your own response, compare it with the one given here.

Remember, though, that there are very few absolutely right or absolutely wrong answers in English. The important thing is for you to be able to back up your answer with evidence from the poem.

The suggestions given here are merely one possible response. There will be others.

Sample 1

> My father worked with a horse-plough,
> His shoulders globed like a full sail strung
> Between the shafts and the furrow.
> The horses strained at his clicking tongue

(From 'Follower' by Seamus Heaney)

Level 1 question

How can you tell that the poet's father is strong and hard working from this stanza?　　(3)

Answer

The father has 'globed' shoulders, suggesting he has bulging muscles. He controls horses that strain 'at his clicking tongue', suggesting they are a good team. Work with the horse plough must be hard, but his father seems used to it.

Level 2 question

What impressions of the poet's father are created in this stanza?　　(4)

Answer

His father is presented as very strong, his shoulders are rounded ('globed') like a billowing sail as he controls his plough horses. He and the horses are a team and they respond by pulling harder ('strained') at the sound of his 'clicking tongue'. The rhyming of 'strung' and 'tongue' and half-rhyming 'plough' and 'furrow' help to reinforce the rhythm of the work of the man and his horses. Although the work is simple and earthy, there is also an elegance and precision to it. The sails in the poet's simile are delicate, which makes for an interesting contrast.

 Revision tip

Read some unfamiliar poems (any anthology will provide some) and think about how you would respond to them in an exam.

Sample 2

> I was angry with my friend
> I told my wrath, my wrath did end
> I was angry with my foe
> I told it not, my wrath did grow.

(From 'A Poison Tree' by William Blake)

Level 1 question

How do you know, from this stanza, that the poet thinks it is better to talk about anger than to say nothing? (2)

Answer

It says that when the man 'told his wrath' it ended, but when he 'told it not' his wrath grew.

Level 2 question

How does the poet communicate his point about anger in this stanza? (3)

Answer

This stanza is like a nursery rhyme or a proverb. It uses very simple language – almost all the words have just one syllable so it is quite childlike – and no imagery or anything sophisticated to say that when he 'told his wrath', or talked about his anger, it disappeared. On the other hand, the second half of the perfectly balanced stanza with its firm rhyming pairs of lines, says that bottled-up anger ('I told it not') will grow, and by implication turn into something more serious. It is significant too that in the first two lines he is thinking about being angry with a friend and in the second two an enemy.

Sample 3

> I leant upon a coppice gate
> When Frost was spectre-gray
> And Winter's dregs made desolate
> The weakening eye of day

(From 'The Darkling Thrush' by Thomas Hardy)

Level 1 question

How can you tell from this stanza that it is late on a winter afternoon? (3)

Answer

First of all the poet tells us the frost is 'spectre-gray'. If frost, which is usually white, is grey then it must be getting darker. Also, the poet talks of the 'weakening' of day. When day grows weak, it means it is ending, so evening is here.

Level 2 question

What atmosphere is created in this stanza? (3)

Answer

It is a late winter's afternoon and it is very cold. The poet is in a rural place, perhaps on the edge of a wood ('coppice gate') and the 'spectre-gray' frost is creating a ghostly atmosphere in the fading light. The metaphorical 'dregs' of winter suggest that this is towards the end of winter – like the last drop in the bottom of a cup or glass. The personification of day with its 'weakening eye' adds to the sense of end-of-the-day gloom and creates a rather despondent mood.

Sample 4

I'll never be a lap dog licking dirty feet,
A sleek dog, a meek dog, cringing for my meat,
Not for me the fireside or the well-filled plate,
But shut door, and sharp stone, and cuff and kick, and hate.

(From 'Lone Dog' by Irene McLeod)

Level 1 question

How can you tell, from this stanza, that the dog narrating the poem is fierce? (2)

Answer

The dog says it will never be a dog 'cringing for my meat', suggesting it is more aggressive and fierce. The dog also says it won't be a lap dog. Lap dogs like comfort, but the dog in the poem obviously doesn't, so it is harder and fiercer.

Level 2 question

How does the poet convey the dog's personality in this stanza? (4)

Answer

The alliterative first line ('lap', 'licking', 'dog', 'dirty') and the internal rhyme of 'sleek' and 'meek' in the second combine with the regular metre and tight end rhymes to make the lines move energetically like a dog running or panting. The use of the negatives 'never' and 'not' introduce a note of pride into the narrative voice. He despises dogs which are 'sleek' or 'meek' and dependent on human beings for a 'well-filled plate'. The repetition of 'and' four times in the fourth line sounds very determined and definite as if the dog is barking out his aggression.

 Revision tip

Choose a short poem from an anthology. Read it carefully. Then write your own six questions based on it. If you do this with a partner you could then swap poems and answer each other's questions as a revision exercise.

3.4 Practice task

Now try this exercise which is similar to a Paper 2 Section A task.

The marks at the end of each question are a guide as to how much you should write in your answers.

You should spend around 35 minutes on the task. Spend the first 5 minutes planning. Write for about 25 minutes. Read your work through in the last 5 minutes to check for mistakes and to make small changes.

There are suggestions to show you how to write good answers in the Answer guidance section, pages 82–84. Do not look at these until you've tried this task yourself. Then consult the suggestions to see how you might have done it better.

'Sunken Evening' by Laurie Lee

The green light floods the city square –
A sea of fowl and feathered fish,
Where squalls of rainbirds dive and splash
And gusty sparrows chop the air.

5 Submerged, the prawn-blue pigeons feed
In sandy grottoes round the Mall,
And crusted lobster-buses crawl
Among the fountains' silver weed.

There, like a wreck, with mast and bell,
10 The torn church settles by the bow,
While phosphorescent starlings stow
Their mussel shells along the hull.

The oyster-poet, drowned but dry,
Rolls a black pearl between his bones;
15 The typist, trapped by telephones,
Gazes in bubbles at the sky.

Till, with the dark, the shallows run,
And homeward surges tide and fret –
The slow night trawls its heavy net
20 And hauls the clerk to Surbiton.

Level 1

1 Look at stanza 3. How can you tell that the starlings are settling down for the night? (1)

2 Look at stanza 4.

Why does the narrator think the typist is trapped? (2)

Why is the poet compared with an oyster? (2)

3 Write two quotations which show that the poet is comparing the city with an underwater scene. (2)

Explain your choices. (4)

4 What changes in the last stanza and how do you know? (4)

5 Write three quotations which show that this poem is set in London. (3)

Explain your choices. (2)

6 How effective do you think the comparison of a busy city with an underwater scene is? (5)

1   Comment on the poet's reference to the 'starlings' in the third stanza.   (3)

2   Explain what the poet is comparing the city with. Refer closely to several words from different stanzas in your answer.   (4)

3   Re-read the fourth stanza. Why does the poet think the typist is trapped? Why is the poet compared with an oyster? Refer closely to the poem to support your ideas.   (4)

4   (a) What changes in the last stanza?   (1)

    (b) How does the poet describe this change?   (2)

5   The poet doesn't tell us the exact place that this poem describes.

    Where do you think it is? Include at least three quotations in your answer.   (6)

6   How effective do you find the poet's use of comparison in this poem? Support your answer by referring closely to the poem.   (5)

★ Make sure you know

★ How to approach the poetry comprehension questions of the 13+ exam.

★ The different techniques which poets use and the names for them.

★ How to use your understanding of these terms in your answers.

★ How to write about the effects these techniques create.

★ How to respond in detail to short sections of a poem and whole poems.

4 Writing for practical purposes

You will be asked to write two compositions in your 13+ Common Entrance exams. This applies to both Level 1 and Level 2 candidates.

Your first writing task is in Paper 1. It gives you the opportunity to show that you can use language to:

- argue
- persuade
- explain
- advise
- inform.

There is also the option, in Paper 1, to demonstrate these skills by writing about one or more novels or other texts (such as a set of short stories, a play, biography or travel book) which you have studied in class or read independently. The examiners will not direct you to write about a specific text. They will, instead, offer you a general writing task which you can apply to any text you have read and chosen to write about.

The reading-related task will give you the opportunity to write about:

- dramatic moments
- episodes in which development and change take place
- contrasts between, for example, characters, places or events
- various other aspects of your chosen text such as themes or settings.

The other options in this section will be tasks similar to the following:

- Write a detailed description of a place which you have visited on holiday in a way which either recommends it warmly or makes it clear that it is not, in your opinion, worth going to.

- Write about an occasion when you were worried or in danger. What did you do and why?

- Think about the advantages and disadvantages of knowledge and ignorance, knowing and not knowing things. Argue in favour of one over the other – with examples.

You might be asked to write your responses in the form of:

- a letter
- an email
- a magazine or newspaper article
- a speech.

Alternatively, you might be allowed to choose the format, in which case you would normally write an essay.

> ## Exercise
>
> For practice, choose one of the ideas described on page 33 – or invent a similar one of your own – and practise with it. Make sure you spend at least 5 minutes planning it and making notes. Allow yourself about 30 minutes' writing time.

4.1 Writing from personal experience

Writing an account of something which has happened to you could include several types of writing. If, for example, you are writing about an accident you have experienced you might also be arguing for better safety procedures or explaining your point of view. Or an account of sports day at school might involve advising schools and teachers how to manage such events better or persuading parents not to embarrass their children.

If you opt for this sort of writing:

● Make it witty if you can.

● Remember that smiling at yourself as you look back often works well.

● Don't be afraid to express yourself in an unusual or original way.

Example of writing from personal experience

Look at this very short extract, from a personal account of a concert which went wrong, as an example:

> *The good news is that I come in bang on time, on the first beat. The bad news is that everyone else is playing the wrong music in the wrong key. This never used to matter when I played keyboard for the Club Symphonique de Limoges with whom we once managed to get through an entire concert with the flautist playing one whole piece ahead of the rest of us.*
>
> *And nobody noticed.*
>
> (Michael Wright, the *Daily Telegraph*, 22 December 2012)

Points to note

The writer:

● uses irony to show that he did not come in at the right time and/or play in tune. He pretends he did and that everyone else in the group was wrong

● makes a joke about an earlier concert which had gone even more disastrously wrong

● is very open about his musical shortcomings

● uses the present tense to give his anecdote immediacy

● varies the length of his sentences.

> **Exam tip**
>
> When you are planning your exam answer, list the points you want to make. Each point may become a paragraph or may be subdivided into shorter paragraphs.

Exercise ✓

Practise your skills by writing a paragraph of your own about an occasion when something went wrong in your life. Try to be witty and limit yourself to four sentences of varying length.

4.2 Writing to argue or persuade

Some writing tasks invite you to write your views on something people disagree about. Often this involves writing persuasively.

For example:

- There has been much debate about what children should and should not eat as a regular part of their diet. What are your own thoughts on this subject?

- Fox hunting has been banned in England. What are your views about this?

- What are your own thoughts on the subject of television?

> *TV rots the senses in the head!*
>
> *It kills the imagination dead!*
>
> *It clogs and clutters up the mind!*
>
> *It makes the child so dull and blind!*
>
> (From *Charlie and the Chocolate Factory* by Roald Dahl, 1964)

Do you agree with this sentiment?

Obviously, if you choose an option such as this you will have a view of your own and the purpose of your writing will be to persuade others to agree with you.

Make your case

The task is to set down what you think and to explain why you think this as persuasively as you can.

When you are planning your writing, note any evidence you can think of to support your views. Your evidence might, for example, be from your own experience, things you have read or heard about in the media (such as newspapers, television or the internet), information you have been given by your teachers or parents, or facts and statistics you have gathered from other sources.

For example, if you are writing about healthy eating, you might mention children you know who eat unusually healthily or unhealthily, facts and figures (if you know them) about children becoming less healthy and fatter because of the food many of them eat, and differences parents and schools can make, with examples.

Or, if you are arguing that there is nothing wrong with children's diets, then mention some supporting evidence to prove your points. And/or you might decide to mention your views about the responsibility adults have towards children's eating and whether or not most of them set a good example. If so, again, you will need some evidence.

Useful words and phrases for opinion essays and other forms of persuasive writing include:

- contend/believe/think/suggest/propose/insist ...

- 'Take the five-a-day' rule...' (at the beginning of a sentence to introduce an example)

- What is more …

- Moreover …

- Nevertheless/nonetheless …

- I would argue …

- Evidence suggests …

- Historically/traditionally …

- In the past …

- Some people think …

- I wonder …

 Revision tip
Newspaper columnists writing persuasively often use the formula of an anecdote followed by evidence. Read as many columns as you can – particularly in the weekend newspapers – as part of your revision.

Start with an anecdote

A piece of writing to persuade or inform often works well if you start with an anecdote (a little story about something which has happened to you or someone you know, or something you saw). You can then widen out your argument with evidence and end with a comment which links the evidence to your anecdote.

Examples of writing to persuade or inform

In this letter to the *Daily Telegraph* (on 27 January 2013), writer Paul Vincent starts with something he has done himself (donated a piano) before approvingly describing a scheme to make use of unwanted pianos:

> *I have put an otherwise unwanted piano in an empty shop in my local town.*
>
> *The Pianos in Accessible New Outlets project is endorsed by our town council and arts centre and provides a community service to anyone wanting to play. The premises are unmanned and users pick up a key from a local bookshop.*

Study this extract from a blog published on the *Independent's* website in November 2012:

> *Every child should spend part of every school day reading silently. Renaissance Reading offers computer-based schemes to encourage that but, although many schools have had some success with these, I find them a bit mechanical and I think you can encourage reading without them.*
>
> *Actually it's easy. All a school has to do is to put books and reading at the centre of what it does. Teachers and other adults in schools should be talking about reading and being seen to read themselves. For at least half an hour a day everyone should read – including the adults. Nothing is more important and example works wonders. Wise teachers let pupils choose their own books and don't worry too much about quality at first. The important thing is to build reading stamina – in a world when there are many distractions.*
>
> (Susan Elkin)

Points to note

The writer:

- uses the first person ('I find' and 'I think') to share her views and make it clear that she is basing what she says on experience

- writes some short sentences for dramatic effect and to make the writing sharp and direct ('Every child should spend part of every day reading silently', 'Actually it's easy'), and is very firm ('Nothing is more important and example works wonders')

- is not afraid to give teachers some strong advice – without being rude ('Teachers and other adults in school should ...' and 'Wise teachers ...')

- moves smoothly from one point to the next.

Look closely at this example of opinion writing which uses a different style from the ones on page 36:

> *I am partial to the occasional bag of crisps. The brand I buy claims to be 'handmade'. How? They sell tons of the things in shops across the land. Am I really supposed to believe that vast teams of workers spend their lives making crisps by hand? Don't they have any machines in their factories? And how do you 'hand make' a crisp anyway? A piece of pottery or a nice hand-knitted sweater perhaps, but a crisp?*
>
> (From *Beyond Words* by John Humphrys, 2006)

Points to note

The writer:

- begins with a clear statement

- draws attention to the word he is querying – 'handmade' – in the second

- ridicules the use of the word 'handmade' by making statements in the form of questions

- is not afraid to use non-grammatical 'sentences' such as the last one

- makes his writing very comfortable and accessible by using relaxed expressions such as 'tons of the things' and 'nice hand-knitted sweater'

- is upbeat and amusing.

> Asking rhetorical questions that make it obvious you and your reader know the answer to them can be a useful way of arguing a point and persuading your reader to your point of view.

Exercise

For practice, choose one of the ideas at the beginning of this section – or invent a similar one of your own – and practise with it. Make sure you spend at least five minutes planning it and making notes. Allow yourself about 30 minutes' writing time.

Some writing tasks invite you to discuss someone else's problem, perhaps in the form of a letter or email. Or, as part of the same question, you could be asked to share information.

For example:

- Explain to a friend in a letter how you have taken up a new hobby, sport or pastime. Tell him or her what the activity involves and give reasons why your friend should join you.

- Write an article for the school magazine, newspaper, newsletter or website to help new pupils. Tell them what they need to know about the school, from a pupil's point of view, and give any advice which you think newcomers need.

- Imagine that someone you know has emailed you for advice about a problem.

  Write your answer.

  When you are sharing information or advising:

- be as clear and concise as you can

- set your points down step by step, perhaps in short paragraphs

- use accurate terminology if your writing relates to a specific activity.

Example of writing to advise or inform

Dear Granny

I'm so glad you have decided to buy a computer. I'm sure you won't regret it and soon you'll be able to email me – and we can exchange messages on Facebook and Twitter. You asked my advice about what sort of computer to buy. Well, I think you have four options to choose from.

First, you could buy a big desktop computer like the one in Dad's study. It would take up a fair amount of room, though, because you'd need a screen, keyboard and computer 'box' which are all separate. You'll need to decide whether you have room for this.

Second, you might consider a laptop like mine. It has a reasonable size screen and keyboard but it's all in one so it doesn't take up much room and you can easily carry it around the house although you might find it rather heavy to take out in a bag.

Third, a netbook might suit you – really just a mini laptop. These are really light and portable and you could carry it around very easily. The best ones have a reasonable size keyboard and a small screen.

Fourth, they're more expensive than small laptops but you could think about a tablet – such as an iPad. They are very portable, fine for email and using the Internet for lots of things. They also act as book readers and excellent cameras. But they don't have a proper keyboard. How much typing are you expecting to do?

Points to note

This is, obviously, part of a letter from a grandchild to a grandmother. Notice that the writer:

- thinks the points through carefully and introduces them with 'First', 'Second', etc.

- shares information but keeps it very basic, assuming that her grandmother knows very little

- uses technical terms (desktop, laptop, iPad) but keeps these to a minimum

- focuses on practical matters such as the space in her grandmother's home

- uses expressions appropriate to advice such as 'might suit you', 'you could', 'you might'

- mentions things she assumes her grandmother will have noticed such as 'the one in Dad's study' as a basic way of explaining to a beginner what a desktop computer is.

> When you write to inform or advise think carefully about who the writing is for and write appropriately for that person

Exercise

For practice, choose one of the ideas at the beginning of this section on page 38 – or invent a similar one of your own – and practise with it. Make sure you spend at least 5 minutes planning it and making notes. Allow yourself about 30 minutes' writing time.

4.4 Writing a book-related composition

As we have seen, one of the writing options in Paper 2 invites you to write about books you have read.

You may base your answer on any book or books you have read in or out of school – and it can be a play text as well as any kind of fiction or non-fiction book.

Remember: the question is always a general one which doesn't specify any particular books. This is so that you can answer it with reference to any book you wish.

At the top of your answer always write the title and author of the book(s) you have chosen to write about.

You are likely to be asked to do some of the following:

- write about the impact a book has had on you

- make general points about reading with reference to books you have read

- write about your experience of reading in various other ways.

Express, compare, state
You will always get higher marks if you:

- express your opinions rather than use too much of your space/time simply retelling the story or describing what the book is about

- compare a book with other books or, for example, a main character from one book with characters from other books. For example:

  Tom from 'Goodnight Mister Tom' is rather like Silas in 'Silas Marner'. Each is a lonely old man who comes to life when a child comes to live with him.

- state your preferences and give reasons for them. For example:

  I admired the characterisation in 'Noughts and Crosses'. Malorie Blackman's decision to have both Sephy and Callum as alternating narrators means that you keep seeing characters such as their parents from different points of view. It makes for a really rounded account of Callum and Sephy and their misunderstandings too.

This explains very specifically what the reader liked about the author's way of telling the story. Do not write:

Noughts and Crosses is a brilliant book with really good characters and I recommend it for people my age.

This says nothing at all about the book, only that the reader liked it. Actually there is no evidence in this sentence that the writer has even read it.

In general, it is probably safer to choose texts you have studied in school rather than those you have read individually at home. If you have worked on something as a class text, your teacher will have helped you to learn more about it. You will have taken part in class discussions and you have probably already done some written work connected with the book as part of your class work. You will, therefore, find it easier to write thoughtfully about it in your exam than if you try to write about something you have read casually and quickly on your own.

 Exam tip
Don't be afraid, if it is appropriate for the task, to mention in your exam a book you did *not* enjoy. As long as you give reasons for your views and preference.

Stick to the book

When you're writing about a book try to avoid loose phrases and statements which don't refer specifically to what is in the text. For example, the following sentences would not add much to your writing and would not get you many marks:

- This is a wonderful book and I have recommended it to all my friends.

- I give this great book five stars.

- I shall never forget this book.

- I couldn't put this book down.

- It's a great page-turner.

- This is the best book I have ever read.

- My mum and dad both think it is a good book too.

- A great book for all ages

Use the content

Think of the content of the book as evidence. Use it and refer to it to support the points you make.

Useful phrases and statements for book-related compositions:

- X is the best of the three books by Y I have read because ...

- B, with its ..., ... plot and ..., ... characters, is ...

- I enjoyed/admired the episode in which ... because ...

- The characters are ...

- The plot is ...

- This play is better than ... because ...

Exam tip

Remember that in an exam you are not trying to 'sell' the book or books to the examiner. Rather, you are trying to show him or her how thoughtfully you have read it and how well you can communicate your ideas about it in writing.

Don't be vague

Avoid vague words like 'good', 'great' and 'wonderful'. Instead use specific words such as 'convincing', 'vulnerable' or 'menacing' to describe characters, or 'twisted', 'satisfying', 'puzzling' or 'well constructed' to describe a plot. If it's a non-fiction book use words like 'informative', 'provocative', 'detailed'.

Refer to the author

Refer to the author in your writing as much as you can. Below are some verbs and phrases to help you comment on what the author is doing.

The author (or use his or her surname):

- presents

- wants us to see that

- leads us to think that

- gives us

- offers us

- seems to think

- has a habit of.

> Look particularly at how the author uses dialogue. What does it add to the story? What does it tell you about the characters?

Example of a book-related essay

This is an example of the sort of Paper 2 essay which will please examiners. It refers to Michelle Magorian's 1981 novel *Goodnight Mister Tom* which many of you will have read. Look at it closely.

Notice how the writer stresses the drama, transition and contrast which he or she finds in the chosen text.

Question

Write about a book which has impressed you and explain why you admire it.

Answer

Goodnight Mister Tom *is a story about the evacuation of children out of London to the safety of the countryside. Although I have read other evacuation stories* (Carrie's War *by Nina Bawden and* Fireweed *by Jill Paton Walsh, for example) this is the one which had the most impact on me.*

That is, I think, mostly because of the strength of the characterisation and the way in which Magorian offers us contrasts and similarities between her characters to reflect upon. For example, Tom is, in some ways, like Willie. He is damaged, troubled and lonely – although much kinder than the villagers initially think he is – and it isn't until he meets, and has to be responsible for, the equally damaged Willie, with his background of abuse, that he finds a real purpose in life. The way in which Tom and Willie gradually change and heal each other is deeply moving, especially at the very end when Willie unthinkingly addresses Tom as Dad and Magorian makes it clear that now these two have each other permanently everything will be all right.

There are other contrasts between characters too. Tom is very different from the only other parent figure Willie has known – his mentally ill mother who has severe religious mania, but also works as a prostitute and beats Willie severely as well as locking him in a cupboard with his doomed baby sister. Willie himself, at first very shy, is also contrasted with the self-assured, theatrical Zach who comes from a middle-class background.

Magorian also makes us strongly aware of the contrast between settings. Willie has come from Deptford, then a poor area in south London. Tom's cottage, the village and the church next door are very rural and there's a strong sense there of pulling together in war. We become aware of just how stark the difference is when Willie's mother summons him home and, worried at not hearing from the boy, Tom goes to London to look for him. The author makes us see the horror of war-torn London from Tom's point of view as he gets caught up in an air raid and, eventually, traces Willie to his mother's home. The third environment is the London hospital where Willie is taken for some pretty horrifying treatment which is forced on him. It too contrasts with both Little Weirwold and the streets of London.

Although there is a story with a happy ending at the heart of this novel, it is neither sentimental nor romantic which is part of its appeal. There is a lot of death in the narrative so it reflects real life – especially in war time. Mrs Hartridge's husband, David, is killed in action. Willie has to come to terms with the tragic death of his always cheerful friend Zach in an air raid and with the death of the baby sister (from neglect) he found back in London as well as his mother's suicide. Magorian also gives us a lovely passage in the churchyard when Tom explains to Willie that his wife, Rachel and their child, died many years before, which explains why he has been so withdrawn and bad-tempered for so long.

Goodnight Mister Tom is a very dramatic story with its quiet interludes, sudden deaths, noisy scenes in London – and the almost constant presence of Tom's faithful, sensitive dog Sammy who is, in effect, another character. This element is part of the reason it is so powerful. It is not surprising that it has been made into both a TV film and a stage play, both of which I've seen but neither has the impact of the book which is so much more detailed.

Points to note
This essay:

- shows a detailed knowledge of *Goodnight Mister Tom*
- provides evidence that the writer has read the book thoughtfully
- compares it with other similar books and with adaptations for stage and screen
- comments on characterisation
- focuses on Magorian's skill in creating interesting contrasts
- tells the examiner how the candidate responds to the book
- is carefully structured with an introduction and conclusion
- demonstrates most of the points made in this chapter about book-related tasks!

Exercise

Write about any book you have read recently. Explain in detail what you thought of it and why.

4.5 Practice tasks

This is an example of the choice you can expect in Paper 1 Section B. Use the tasks for practice.

You should spend around 40 minutes in total on each task. Spend the first 5 minutes planning.

Write for about 30 minutes. Read your work through in the last 5 minutes to check for mistakes and to make small changes.

1 A difficult decision.

Was there a time when you had to make a difficult decision? How did you eventually decide what to do?

Write about it in the form of an email to a friend.

2 Sport in school should be optional.

Imagine you are taking part in a debate with this statement as the proposal.

Write a speech in which you argue either for or against it.

3 Think about a time when you, or a member of your family, did something you later regretted. Describe it in an entertaining and humorous way.

4 EITHER

a) 'Books are uniquely portable magic.' (Stephen King)

Have you ever read a book, fiction or non-fiction, which for you was 'portable magic'?

Explain why it impressed you so much.

OR

b) 'A really good book needs three things: strong characters, a good plot and something to make you think.'

Explain how far you agree with this statement by referring to your own reading.

★ Make sure you know

★ How to write from personal experience.

★ How to write to argue or persuade.

★ How to write to advise, inform or explain.

★ How to write a book-related composition.

5 Creative writing

Paper 2 invites you to write in an original, fictional, imaginative way.

This chapter therefore looks at some of the general skills that are required for writing well and then goes on to focus on the skills you need for writing stories and descriptions, including how to create convincing characters and dialogue.

Paper 2 will give you a choice of subjects to write about. The paper usually includes options such as:

- a story

- an imaginative description

- a quotation, statement or title which you can respond to in any imaginative way you wish.

 Exam tip

Remember that with the third option above you are free to write in any way you wish but your use of language needs to be appropriate and accurate.

You must choose *one* of these. The same options for writing are offered at both levels.

The examiner wants you to be as free as possible to show how well you can use language imaginatively to write descriptively and to tell stories. That is why the suggestions you are given to choose from are quite vague and open ended.

It is important that you:

- write in an appropriate way for the task you have chosen

- spell correctly

- punctuate and use grammar properly

- use exciting vocabulary accurately.

5.1 Writing well

Here are some practical ideas to help you improve the quality of your writing.

 Revision tip

As you revise, try writing paragraphs with sentences of different lengths. Look out for sentences of different lengths while you're reading too.

Sentence length
Vary the length of your sentences. A piece of writing in which all the sentences are roughly the same length is usually dull and flat.

Look at an example of a professional writer using sentences of different lengths:

> *Her beauty silenced us. Despite Kenji's enthusiasm earlier, I was quite unprepared for it. I thought then that I understood Lady Maruyana's suffering: at least part of it had to be jealousy. How could any man refuse the possession of such beauty?*
>
> (From *Across the Nightingale Floor* by Lian Hearn, 2002)

In one paragraph Lian Hearn has a sequence of sentences which have – in order – 4, 10, 18 and 10 words. Read it aloud. You will notice that varied sentence and word length creates rhythm, which matters as much in prose as in poetry. The stresses in the words rise and fall in an irregular way but the writing sounds complete and elegant because of its prose rhythm.

One technique is to build a paragraph of three sentences, each one shorter than the one before. It is quite dramatic and makes your reader want to hurry on to the next paragraph. Here is an example of a professional writer using this technique:

> *Becky knew her tirade had gone too far, that she'd spoiled the day, that it would make her mother cry, and that she'd hate herself later for making her unhappy again. But to her surprise, her mother didn't cry this time. Instead she went very quiet.*
>
> (From *Best Mates* by Michael Morpurgo, 2007)

Sentence shape

Make sure that you vary the shapes of your sentences too. If you are writing a story about Josh don't start the first five sentences with 'Josh' or 'he' followed by a verb.

Instead:

- Start sometimes with a fronted clause or phrase, for example:

  Knowing that he was already late, Josh …

  Desperate and angry, Josh …

- Write an occasional 'inside out' sentence. So, instead of:

  Josh ran as fast as he could because Mia was in terrible danger.

  write:

  Because he knew Mia was in terrible danger, Josh ran as fast as he could.

- If you're writing conversation, vary the position of the words which explain who is speaking (the speech tags). They can go at the beginning, in the middle or at the end of spoken words. Change the order of them too. Use 'Martha said' as well as 'said Martha':

  Freddy said, 'I don't believe a word of it. It just can't be true.'

  'I don't believe a word of it. It just can't be true,' said Freddy.

  'I don't believe a word of it,' said Freddy. 'It just can't be true.'

- Stir some indirect speech into the mix of conversation too:

  Freddy said he didn't believe a word of it because it just couldn't be true.

- Start some sentences with adverbs such as 'hurriedly', 'anxiously', 'now' or 'there', for example:

There, in the garden, Felicity waited.

Hurriedly, he leapt on his bike and began to pedal.

- Experiment occasionally with putting the verb before the subject in some of your sentences. For example:

Suddenly, up jumped the dog.

Downhill marched the group towards the village.

Study this example of a professional writer varying the shape of her sentences:

> *Uncle Acquila lived on the extreme edge of Calleva. One reached his house down a narrow side street that turned off not far from the East Gate, leaving behind the forum and the temples, and coming to a quiet angle of the old British earthworks – for Calleva had been a British Dun before it became a Roman city – where the hawthorn and hazel still grew and the shyer woodland birds still came. It was much like the other houses of Calleva, timbered and red-roofed and comfortable, built round three sides of a tiny courtyard that was smoothly turfed and set about with imported roses and gum-cistus growing in tall stone jars. But it had one peculiarity: a squat, square, flat-roofed tower rising from one corner: for Uncle Acquila. Having lived most of his life in the shadow of watch-towers from Memphis to Segedunum, he could not be comfortable without one.*

(From *The Eagle of the Ninth* by Rosemary Sutcliff, 1954)

Rosemary Sutcliff uses compound and complex sentences (interspersed with simple ones like the one which opens her paragraph) and often punctuates them with colons and semi-colons.

Note: Colons are used to indicate that another statement is following. Semi-colons are sometimes used in place of full stops or commas to divide two balanced sentences, or longer items in a list. (For more on colons and semi-colons, see Chapter 6.)

 Revision tip

As you revise, practise writing paragraphs consisting of sentences of different shapes. Notice and think about sentence shape while you're reading too.

Verbs and nouns, adverbs and adjectives

It is not usually good style to clutter your writing with too many adjectives and adverbs or descriptive clauses. Instead, choose strong and appropriate verbs and nouns.

Use adverbs and adjectives only if they are really necessary or add something.

In each of the following examples, the first sentence is much better than the second:

1 The water <u>trickled</u> along the <u>gully</u>.

2 A *small* amount of water ran *slowly* along the bottom of the *steep little* valley.

1 <u>Musicologists</u> have found the <u>manuscript</u> of one of Beethoven's <u>overtures</u> in an <u>attic</u> in Vienna.

2 *Music* experts have found Beethoven's *original handwritten* copy of one of his *short* pieces in a *top-floor* room in Vienna.

1 When she heard the fire alarm, Amelia <u>stiffened</u>.

2 When she heard the fire alarm, Amelia felt *nervous* and *worried*.

1 Goliath <u>strode</u> towards David.

2 Goliath walked *determinedly with big steps* towards David.

(Strong, appropriate nouns and verbs are underlined. Avoidable adjectives and adverbs are in *italics*.)

> Using strong verbs and nouns usually means shorter sentences too – which helps you to vary the shape of your sentences.

Avoid using adjectives and adverbs that add nothing to your writing. They can even weaken the effect of a strong verb or noun.

In the following examples, the first option is stronger and clearer and therefore carries more weight:

1 I am exhausted.

2 I am really exhausted.

1 He apologised.

2 He apologised very sincerely.

If you feel tempted to use the adverb 'actually', or the adjective 'actual', ask yourself if you really need it. Try your sentence without it. You may be surprised how well it works when it is free of these 'clutter' words.

> Make a mental list of adjectives and adverbs which you rarely need. Start it with: very, actually, extremely, awfully …

Repetition

Apart from words such as 'and' and 'the', try to avoid repeating words in your writing. Look at this example:

> *At moonrise I walked on, not ceasing until I at last reached the foot of the Black Mountains. Here I settled, and chewed upon more of Dahtet's dried meat. Then I lay upon the dusty ground that I might refresh my body with some little sleep. Across the flat land Golahka would come at dawn, and this time I knew he would cross swiftly meaning to reach our camp before I did.*
>
> (From *Apache* by Tanya Landman, 2007)

The writer uses 'cross' to avoid repeating 'walked' or 'walk'. 'Ceasing', 'settled' and 'lay' all have a sense of stopping to rest but there is no repetition.

The better your vocabulary, the easier it is to write fluently.

 Revision tip

A good personal word bank comes from reading widely, so make sure you continue to read as many books as you can even while you are revising.

If you're writing about people, try not to repeat their names more often than necessary. Of course you can use pronouns such as 'he', 'she' or 'they' but take care that it's clear exactly to whom they refer.

For occasional variety use words and phrases to refer to your characters such as:

- the boy/girl/man/woman
- the pupil/child/student
- the teacher/lorry driver/solicitor (or any other profession)
- her/his friend
- our neighbour.

Tautology

Overuse of adjectives and adverbs often leads to tautology – unnecessary repetition.

Do not, for example, write:

- return back – 'return' means to go or to give back so the adverb 'back' is tautological
- ascend up – 'ascend' means to go up
- reply back – 'reply' means to speak or write back.

 Revision tip

As you revise, make your own list of common tautologies to avoid.

Exercise 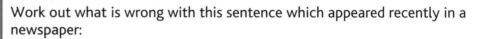 ✓

Work out what is wrong with this sentence which appeared recently in a newspaper:

President Chen says the government of Taiwan plans to re-apply for UN membership again in the future.

Paragraphing

A paragraph is, of course, a group of sentences within a piece of prose writing (i.e. not poetry or a play) that are grouped together and separated from the rest of the writing. A paragraph can sometimes consist of a single sentence and occasionally – usually for dramatic effect – a single word.

Begin a new paragraph when:

- you introduce a new topic, idea, character or opinion
- a new person speaks in a passage of dialogue in a story
- you want to create a dramatic effect.

Remember:

- in modern writing long, wandering paragraphs are generally regarded as weak style (although nineteenth-century writers such as Jane Austen and Charles Dickens loved them); three or four sentences is usually an ideal
- good paragraphing shows the examiner that you can organise your ideas in writing – which is one of the main things looked for in this exam
- if in doubt, begin a new paragraph
- a one-sentence or even a one-word paragraph can be a useful way of making your writing dramatic or capturing your reader's interest.

5.2 Writing stories

One of the options in Paper 2 is usually to write a story. This requires some thought before you start about how the story will begin, develop and end, and the style in which you will write. The section on creating characters (see pages 51–52) will also help you to write a good story.

Plan your story

Plan your story so that you know where it's going. Never try, in an exam, to make up a story as you go along. Spend about 5 minutes creating your plan.

For example, if you were asked to write a story which begins with a telephone conversation, your plan might look like this:

1 Mother and TV presenter talking on the phone. Competition results. Child has won trip to Antarctica.

2 Mother off phone – her feelings.

3 Flashback to advertisement for the competition and entering it. Child's very strong ambition to see Antarctica.

4 Some time later. Setting off for the trip – airport. Meeting rest of group. Excitement.

Once you have an outline plan of your story, you can fill in the details as you write. For the example above, you would need to think about the following:

● Is the child a boy or a girl?

● How old is he/she?

● What is his/her name?

● What did entering the competition involve?

● Why is he/she keen to go to Antarctica? Has he/she read a lot about it or seen television documentaries? Was his/her great-great-grandparent an explorer?

Exercise

Try the sample question above for yourself. Either use the plan given or devise a completely different plan of your own. Allow yourself about 30 minutes' writing time.

Beginnings and endings

Think for a moment about any traditional fairy story. It begins 'Once upon a time ...' and it ends 'And they all lived happily ever after.' Anything that happens between these is the middle of the story.

Your story will, almost certainly, be more complex than a fairy story, but the examiner is still looking for an effective opening and a rounded-off ending. Think of these as the frame which encloses your story.

There are many ways of starting a story. For example, you can:

● Introduce a character. For example:

Fergus was sitting on the sea wall idly drumming his heels ...

● Set the scene. For example:

The bell rang and Year 6 erupted noisily through the damp, grey walled area into the panelled hall where hot chocolate and buns awaited them ...

- Describe a situation in which everything is not quite what it seems, to tantalise your reader. Then in the next paragraph you explain what is really happening. For example:

They were being attacked on all sides. The noise rattled over their heads. Adrenaline had never been higher. This was life and death ... James and Abdullah had always loved football. It was what cemented their friendship ...

- Jump straight into unexplained dialogue and later explain who is speaking and why. For example:

'Let's go inside and find out.'

'Do you really think we should?'

'Yes, come on.'

Hannah and Jessica were standing outside Horniman's Museum in London. Hannah was insisting that one of the exhibits was a famous stuffed walrus. Jessica was sceptical.

- Make a mysterious statement to entice the reader to read on. For example:

It was all Shakespeare's fault ...

I have always adored apricot jam ...

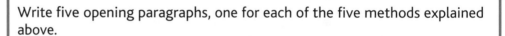

Exercise ✔

Write five opening paragraphs, one for each of the five methods explained above.

Another way to begin, if you find it very difficult to write a complete story in just over half an hour, is to imagine that you are writing two or three pages from the *middle* of an exciting, gripping, interesting or moving book.

This means you don't have to worry so much about balanced and satisfying beginnings and endings. You can concentrate instead on making your writing as lively as possible.

If you decide to do this in your exam, you will need to:

- Plan your writing just as carefully as if you were producing a complete story.

- State clearly at the top that this is a passage extracted from an imaginary book.

- Give your imagined novel a title.

- Write a one- or two-sentence introduction at the top similar to the explanations teachers and examiners put in front of passages taken from books for comprehension work.

- Try to end on an exciting 'cliff hanger' to tantalise the reader.

You can end your story in different ways too. For instance, you might:

- Spring a surprise. End with something the reader was not expecting. For example, if two characters have been exploring a cave your reader is probably waiting for them to discover something interesting and come out safe at the end. Instead you could drown them as the tide comes in. If you write a love story you might end with the two people separating without the obvious 'happy ever after' ending.

- Take your characters back to where they started. So, for example, have your character sitting on the sea wall at the end of the story as he was at the beginning.

- End with a joke. For example:

The moral of this story is that parents are better news than you might think.

And so, you see, it isn't usually a good idea to pit yourself against a challenge – whatever teachers, pushy parents and youth leaders might tell you.

Avoid the following:

- Endings that have been done far too often before and will make the examiner sigh in exasperation. For example, the narrator waking up at the end and revealing it was all a dream, or revealing that the mystery character sighted earlier (perhaps on a roadside) is the ghost of someone who died there a while ago.

- Tailing off without a definite ending.

 Exam tip
Strong beginnings and endings almost always mean a well-written, gripping story likely to attract high marks in an examination.

Using the first or third person

Most stories are told by:
- a narrator who describes from the outside what is happening to characters and refers to them as 'he', 'she' or 'they' – known grammatically as the third person

or:
- a character who is part of the story him or herself so there is an 'I' – or first person – in the story.

Before you start to write your story, you must decide whether you are going to write it in the first person or the third person.

Even if you opt for the third person you are quite likely to present what happens through the eyes of one character. An example of this is Becky in the extract by Michael Morpurgo on page 45.

Once you have made up your mind who is telling your story, it is essential that you stick to it. Stories which begin in the third person and then slip into the first by mistake go badly wrong and lose many marks.

Exercise

Write two paragraphs from different stories, one in the first person and the other in the third.

5.3 Creating characters

There are some key points to remember when creating your characters and writing their dialogue.

Interesting characters

Make sure your story includes some colourful characters but do not try to include too many. Although some novels have dozens of characters, the story that you write in your exam will be very short so you do not have space for more than two or three main characters. If you try to include more, your story will be confused and confusing.

Present each character in as much detail as you can. Show him or her doing and saying things as a way of communicating to your reader what the character is like. This is usually more effective than just telling the reader what the character is like.

In each of these examples, the first option is more effective than the second:

1 Sophie was curled up on the settee reading *David Copperfield* by Charles Dickens.

2 Sophie is an intelligent girl who loves books.

1 As Jake opened his birthday card from his grandmother, a cheque for £500 fell on to the floor.

2 Jake's grandmother is very well off.

Characters' names

Give the characters in your story believable names. In real life a person's name is usually related to one or more of the following:

● The period in which he or she was born. In the early twentieth century many babies were given names such as Albert, Doris, Phyllis and Vera. In the middle of the twentieth century Susan, David, Peter and Anne were popular. By the 1990s, it was Oliver, Chloe, Charlotte and Ben. Some names, of course, move in and out of fashion. Old names such as George, Henry, Florence and Beatrice are popular again now.

● The country he or she comes from. Names such as Callum and Douglas are Scottish. Huw and Gwyneth are Welsh names. Names such as Eva, Elena and Nicolas (spelt without the 'h') are popular in many European countries. You can also use ethnically diverse names when portraying characters from different backgrounds.

● His or her social class. In the early twentieth century someone called Violet was more likely to be a servant than a girl named Alexandra. A boy named Ron was more likely to work in, say, a coal mine, than a young man called Julian.

Your story will ring much truer if you give your characters appropriate names. Think about the names of the people you know – the very elderly, the middle-aged, younger people and anyone you know who comes (or whose family comes) from outside Britain.

Dialogue

Dialogue can be used to show what characters are like too. Let your characters introduce themselves to your reader through what they say. This is what happens in real life and so it works well in stories.

Look, for example, at how the caring, respectful side of Hazel's character is shown in the words he uses in this extract. Note that Hazel is a rabbit, speaking to his brother, Fiver:

> *'You don't suppose I'll leave you to look after yourself, do you?' said Hazel. 'But to tell you the truth, I sometimes feel like clearing out of this warren altogether. Still, let's forget it now and try to enjoy the evening. I'll tell you what – shall we go across the brook? There'll be fewer rabbits there and we can have a bit of peace. Unless you feel it isn't safe?' he added.*

> (From *Watership Down* by Richard Adams, 1972)

Here's another example which is written as a first person narrative. Look at how much you learn about the narrator from what the author makes her say here, near the beginning of the book:

> *I checked my nails, smoothed down my pinafore and sniffed. I was not used to being right inside the house and the air seemed to close about me stiflingly, an inside sort of air, stuffy and tickling my nose, a mixture of the previous night's coal fires, the fibres of the thick wool carpets and the scent from the bowl of dried rose petals on the hall table.*
>
> (From *The Disgrace of Kitty Grey* by Mary Hooper, 2013)

Exercise

Write a paragraph or two of dialogue in which your character or characters begin to reveal what they think or feel or what their personalities are like.

When you are writing dialogue try to make it more interesting and less repetitive by using words other than 'said' to explain who is speaking. There are many other possibilities, some of them quite colourful, such as:

asked	exclaimed	muttered
bellowed	groaned	proposed
breathed	growled	questioned
declaimed	grumbled	shouted
demanded	mumbled	suggested
enquired	murmured	whispered

 Revision tip

As part of your revision, create a list of words to use when you are writing dialogue. Add to the list any words for 'said' you come across in your reading.

Sometimes, if two characters are speaking alternately in short sentences, you don't need explanatory words to tell the reader who is speaking. This has the effect of making the dialogue run very fast down the page and is good, for example, for arguments.

For example:

> *'Look what I've got,' she said, waving it at me, like a baby-faced assassin.*
>
> *'What is it like?'*
>
> *'What does it look like?'*
>
> *'And where did you find it?'*
>
> *'Sue gave it to me.'*
>
> *It felt so good to be having a conversation with her ...*
>
> (From *Firewallers* by Simon Packham, 2013)

5.4 Writing descriptions

A description is, for the purposes of this exam, a piece of imaginative writing which describes, say, a person, place or event without the full plot you would create in a story.

For example, if you were given the subject 'the beach' and decided to write a description rather than a story you might imagine and write about:

- a lonely, sandy beach along a bay at dawn
- the smell and sounds
- huge waves
- two surfers arriving in the distance and starting to ride the waves
- one man with a dog on the beach
- seabirds searching for worms
- ships out at sea
- the atmosphere including the light.

Or, if you wanted to write a description in response to the subject 'the old man', you might simply create a character and describe him as if you were introducing him to the reader. You might describe his:

- appearance
- manner
- home
- dog
- family
- background
- likes and dislikes
- habits.

You should be sure to make him as unusual and interesting as possible.

 Exam tip

Remember that almost all stories and novels use description as part of the storytelling. The descriptions are woven into the text alongside dialogue. If you write a description in your exam, think of it as an extract from a novel. But remember not to include plot elements in your description as these will turn it into a narrative.

Beginning

You should begin your writing with a strong statement which will make your reader want to read on. For example:

- My Uncle Joe is a puppeteer.
- Everyone in my family has childhood memories of Bournemouth since my great-great-grandfather bought a holiday home there in 1921.
- I was in the water. It was deep and cold. I was fully dressed. There was no one in sight.

Using your senses

Use all five of your senses to bring your writing to life. Write about what you can:

- hear, for example the waves on that beach
- smell, for example the seaweed

- taste, for example the salt on your lips

- feel, for example the sand beneath your feet

- see – this is the most obvious one.

Using your memories

Use your memories and make them as entertaining as you can. You might, for example, remember a special holiday, visiting a relative or a time when something interesting, funny, sad or silly happened to you.

Using metaphors and similes

Use interesting – and original – metaphors and similes. They will make your writing more vivid, exciting and memorable.

In each of these examples, the first option is more effective than the second:

1 She felt as if she was standing on the edge of a perilous precipice.

2 She was scared.

1 I fell upon my food like a starving hyena.

2 I ate my lunch hungrily.

1 My mother is an inspired and enthusiastic artist in the kitchen, mixing a fabulous palate of tastes and textures in her pans and pots.

2 My mother is a good cook.

5.5 Practice tasks

This is an example of the choice you can expect in Paper 2 Section B. Use the tasks for practice.

You should spend around 40 minutes in total on each task. Spend the first 5 minutes planning. Write for about 30 minutes. Read your work through in the last 5 minutes to check for mistakes and to make small changes.

> **?**
>
> 1 Write a story or a description using one of the following titles:
>
>   a) A surprise
>
>   b) The visit to the castle
>
>   c) Shopping
>
> 2 'It is never too late.'
>
>   Write about this in any imaginative way you wish.
>
> 3 'Did you do this?'
>
>   'Yes and I'll tell you why.'
>
>   Write a story which includes these two lines of dialogue.
>
> 4 Reaching the top
>
>   Use this title to write a description or story.

★ Make sure you know

★ How to write well.

★ How to write engaging stories.

★ How to create well-constructed, credible characters.

★ How to write vivid and detailed descriptions.

6 Grammar, punctuation and spelling

Your 13+ English exams involve reading carefully, writing perceptive answers and producing imaginative or well-reasoned essays.

A sound knowledge of the basic 'nuts and bolts' of English will help you to do all of that with precision. Usually grammar, punctuation and spelling are not marked separately – although some senior schools choose to give a separate mark out of 10 for grammar which often includes punctuation and spelling. This would mean that if you write imaginatively and have a good vocabulary but have, for example, a spelling learning difficulty the examiner will give you the marks you deserve for your ideas without being put off by your spelling.

In most cases, however, your grammar, punctuation and spelling are marked along with the content you write. It is part of the general impression your work gives the examiner – and an important part. You will *not* be asked specific questions about grammar (or punctuation or spelling) in your papers.

> Pay close attention to grammar, punctuation and spelling because they underpin everything you write. Just as a building will collapse if its foundations are not properly built so your writing may be seriously weakened by poor grammar, punctuation and spelling.

 Revision tip

Revise the technicalities of English thoroughly so that you make as few mistakes as possible in your writing. Errors will cost you marks.

6.1 Word classes or 'parts of speech'

There are at least two good reasons for knowing the main word classes:

- If you have good background knowledge of the shape of sentences and the different sorts of words which go into a good one you are more likely to be able to construct sentences which convey their meaning clearly and effectively.

- It can be useful to use the vocabulary of grammar in a comprehension answer. You might write for example:

  - The poet's use of aggressive verbs ...

  - The effect of the author's list of abstract nouns suggests ...

Here is a brief summary of the parts of speech and how they work.

Remember that words are not loyal. They belong to different groups depending on the job they are required to do in a particular sentence. So concentrate on what sort of a word it is in the sentence you are writing or studying. Don't worry about what sort of word it might be in a different context.

Nouns

A noun is a naming word. There are several sorts:

- Common – for example: chair, computer, house, boy
- Proper – for example: Edinburgh, Prince Harry, Pizza Express, River Mersey
- Abstract – for example: adoration, anger, thirst, carelessness
- Collective – for example: herd (of cattle), pack (of cards), flock (of birds or sheep)

Revision tip

Try to revise one of the eight parts of speech covered here each day. Make up more examples as part of your revision. Tick off each word class when you are sure you understand it.

Verbs

Verbs are the action or 'being' words which show you what is happening in a sentence.

- We **walked** all the way to town.
- Mr Smith **is** our teacher.
- '**Run** faster!' **shouted** the cricket coach.
- We **are** the champions.

Verbs can be expressed in various versions of the past, present and future tenses, depending on when the action or situation took, takes or will take, place.

In sentences verbs often consist of several words because they sometimes use auxiliary (helping) verbs – **to have** or **to be** – to show the tense.

- In October we **shall have been living** in our house for ten years.
- I **was wandering** along the corridor.
- You **will be** late for school.
- **Has** she **been reading** *Harry Potter and the Philosopher's Stone*?

Adjectives

Adjectives are describing words which 'qualify' or 'modify' – or tell you more about – nouns.

- I love **hot**, **sunny** days.
- Drink your tea before it gets **cold**.
- **Red** roses are my **favourite** flowers.

They can be used in a comparative (more) form: hotter, more exciting, better.

Or a superlative (most) form: hottest, most exciting, best.

Adverbs

Adverbs are describing words which 'qualify' or 'modify' – or tell you more about – verbs.

They usually tell you how, when, where or why something happens.

- Oliver Twist and his friends ate **hungrily**.
- My horse **rapidly** overtook hers.

- Let's do it **now**.
- Snow lay **everywhere**.

  Adverbs also sometimes qualify other adverbs or adjectives.

- We thought it was best to get there **quite** quickly.
- The girl was **unusually** small.

> Think of an adverb as an add-verb because it **adds** to the meaning of the **verb**, but be careful to spell **adverb** correctly.

Pronouns

Pronouns stand in the place of nouns. They enable you to avoid clumsy repetition of the nouns in your sentences.

There are several sorts:

- Personal

  - I, you, he, she, it, we, they (when it's the subject of the verb). For example:

    He and **I** went swimming.

  - him, her, it, us, them (when it's the object or 'receiver' of the verb). For example:

    Mrs Wentworth told **us** what to do.

- Demonstrative – this dog, that pencil. Such pronouns often drop the accompanying noun. For example:

  - I can't believe **this.**

  - **That** is sharp.

- Possessive – my, mine, your, yours, his, her, hers, its, our, ours, their, theirs. For example:

  - **Her** book is very absorbing.

  - The book is **his.**

  - The building is **our** house.

  - The house is **ours.**

- Relative – who, which, whom, whose. For example:

  - My cousin, **whom** you don't know, lives in Cornwall.

  - This is the book **which** I was telling you about.

  In these examples the pronoun stands for 'my cousin' and 'the book'. Take particular care with 'who' and 'whom'.

- 'Whom' is used when it is standing as the object of a verb or when it follows prepositions (for example to, by, of, through, from, by, at).

  We use 'whom' when, in a differently structured variation of the sentence, we would use 'him' (not 'he'). For example:

  - This is the man **whom** my sister loves. (She loves **him.**)

  - This is the teacher from **whom** I learnt French last year. (I learnt it from **her.**)

- This is the boy with **whom** I went on a Scout camp. (I went with **him**.)
- To **whom** does this pencil case belong? (Does it belong to **her**?)

● 'Who' is used when it is standing as the subject of the verb. We use 'who' when, in other circumstances, we would say 'he'. For example:

- This is the man **who** loves my sister. (**He** loves her.)
- This is the teacher **who** taught me French last year. (**She** taught me.)
- This is the boy **who** went with me on a Scout camp. (**He** went with me.)
- **Who** owns this pencil case? (**She** owns it.)

Prepositions

Prepositions usually tell you the position of something in relation to something else.

● The jam is **in** the cupboard.

● **Under** the apple tree Felix is asleep.

● The dish ran away **with** the spoon.

> Think of prepositions as place words – p for place and p for preposition.

Other prepositions include: within, inside, outside, over, beneath, above, around, up, down, into, with, at.

But many of these words can, as so often in English, also be used to do other jobs in sentences when they are not being prepositions. For more help with this see the section on 'Words doing many jobs' on page 60.

Conjunctions

Conjunctions are joining words.

They can be used to join short sentences to create longer ones or sometimes to hook words together.

> To remember what conjunctions do, think of the **junction** on a railway where two or more lines join.

Common everyday conjunctions include: and, or, because, as, although, but, though, so. For example:

● The prize went jointly to Marina **and** Oliver.

● I like peas **and** so does my brother. (I like peas. My brother does too.)

● I am going fishing at the weekend **because** it is my favourite activity. (I am going fishing at the weekend. It is my favourite activity.)

Like prepositions, conjunctions are slippery little words. The same words often get into sentences doing other jobs. Look, as ever, at *how* they are used before you decide what they are.

Exercise

Try writing a number of short sentences (which follow on logically from each other). Then join them all up into one long sentence, using conjunctions. For example: 'I don't like broccoli. I eat it. It's good for me.' There are several ways you could organise this into one long sentence.

Articles

'The' is the definite article and refers to something specific. For example:

● **the** government

● **the** sea.

Each of these refers to a specific one.
'A' is the indefinite article. For example:

● **a** fox

● **a** poem.

These are not specific because they refer to any fox or poem.
'An' is a form of the indefinite article used when the next word begins with a vowel. For example:

● **an** elephant

● **an** apple

● **an** old coat.

Words doing many jobs

Some words can act as different parts of speech in different sentences.
Take the word 'up', for example:

● Where is the **up** escalator? (adjective)

● We all have our ups and downs and just now I'm enjoying an **up**. (noun)

● The village is **up** there. (preposition)

● I often walk **up** steps because it is good exercise. (adverb)

> The best way of really making sure you have grasped a grammar point is to teach it to someone else.

Exercise

Try using these words as different parts of speech in different sentences: break, fast, as, set, down – and/or think of some other words that you could use in this way. Then try explaining what you've done to someone who doesn't quite understand it.

6.2 Punctuation

This is a summary of the most important uses of the main punctuation marks used in English.

It's important to get your punctuation right, because punctuation marks can change the meaning of a sentence. Incorrect punctuation can therefore confuse your examiner.

Ending a sentence

End every sentence with a full stop (.)

Sometimes it is appropriate to use a question mark (?) or exclamation mark (!) both of which include a full stop.

Do *not* end a sentence with a comma.

Study these two extracts from Ernest Hemingway's short story 'Indian Camp' for correct use of the full stop as a sentence ending. Notice how short some of the sentences are:

> *The two boats started off in the dark. Nick heard the oar-locks of the other boat quite a long way ahead of them in the mist. The Indians rowed with short choppy strokes. Nick lay back with his father's arm around him. It was cold on the water.*
>
> *...*
>
> *Across the bay they found the other boat beached. Uncle George was smoking a cigar in the dark. The young Indian pulled the boat way up the beach. Uncle George gave both the Indians cigars.*

Use a question mark if a question is being asked. For example:

- How far is it to York?
- Are we nearly there?

Use an exclamation mark if you want to turn something you've written into a joke or to make an exclamation dramatic. For example:

- Help!
- Oh my goodness!

Generally it is bad style, and lazy, to use exclamation marks other than very occasionally.

If your choice of words is strong enough, exclamation marks are usually unnecessary. Think how rarely you see them in newspapers, information books or in good novels (except sometimes in dialogue).

Commas

Commas are used inside sentences. Their job is to make meaning clear.

They mark a natural break in the sentence or they separate one part of it from another part. For example:

- Abdul, bring me your homework.
- Put that parcel over there, please.
- A tall man, Mr Smith pulled the book from the top shelf.

They are used to separate items in a list within a sentence. For example:

- Dogs, cats, guinea pigs, hamsters and rabbits all make good pets.
- I've read three books by Dickens, two by Jane Austen, two by Elizabeth Gaskell and one by Thomas Hardy.
- Excited, nervous, exhilarated and passionate, she burst through the door.

Commas are also used in pairs to separate an aside or an extra piece of information from the main thrust of the sentence. For example:

- It is unlikely, however, to happen.
- Nick Wilkins, a professor of English, told the group about studying the subject at university.
- Adela, who is new to our school, is outstanding at maths.

Colons

The colon means 'as follows' or 'like this'. We often use it in this book to follow the words 'for example'. It often precedes lists. For example:

● These are my favourite animals: panda, zebra and hippopotamus.

● This is my opinion: private individuals should not be allowed to own guns.

The colon is not followed by a capital letter unless the word happens to require a capital letter.

Semi-colons

The semi-colon can be used in long complicated lists between commas for clarity. Here is a simple list:

● I bought apples, bananas, oranges and plums.

Semi-colons can be used to expand it into a much longer sentence like this:

● I bought apples, both green and red because we all like different types; bananas which are Dad's favourite, although they sometimes give him indigestion; several sorts of orange, including navels, blood, satsumas and mandarins, and plums.

Semi-colons can also be used in place of commas or full stops for additional emphasis. For example, see the extract on page 8 from *Set in Stone* by Linda Newbery.

Speech marks

Also sometimes called inverted commas or quotation marks (" " or ' '), speech marks always work in pairs. They separate a group of spoken or quoted words from the rest of the sentence.

A capital letter is used each time speech marks are opened unless the speaker is in the middle of a sentence. For example:

● The headmistress said, 'Let us pray.'

● 'Don't you think,' continued Mary, 'that we should ask permission first?'

A comma is usually used at the end of the spoken words inside the speech marks before the writer explains who is speaking. For example:

● 'Let's go,' said Tariq.

● 'That's very interesting,' observed Latifa.

If a full stop, question mark or exclamation mark comes at the end of a spoken sentence it goes inside the speech marks. For example:

● 'Really?' asked Alex.

● 'Wow!' breathed Niamh.

A new paragraph begins each time a different character speaks. Study this piece of dialogue as a way of revising speech marks:

> 'Mr Farrow?' he repeated. 'And he, I assume, has sent you to find me for some reason?'
>
> 'No,' I assured him. 'I have come of my own accord. I am a great admirer of your work, Mr Waring – indeed I am fascinated by it.'
>
> He nodded, seeming to accept this as his due.
>
> 'I have been curious to meet you,' I continued, 'from the first time I set eyes on your wind carvings.'
>
> (From *Set in Stone* by Linda Newbery, 2006)

It doesn't matter whether you use single speech marks (' ') or doubles (" ") but you must be consistent.

If you need to use speech marks within a passage that is itself in speech marks use the type that you have not already used. This gives one of the following patterns:

- 'Fred shouted "Help!" until someone heard.'
- "Fred shouted 'Help!' until someone heard."

Study this example:

> *'No.' Obi gestured at the browser window in front of him. 'With just a name, the births, deaths and marriages database was no help. "Brett Peters" returned, like, a million results.'*
>
> (From *Urban Outlaws Counterstrike* by Peter Jay Black, 2016)

Apostrophes

The apostrophe has two uses. It shows:

- possession
- that letters have been missed out (omission).

Possession

When the possessor is singular the apostrophe goes before the s:

- Bernard's dog is the dog possessed by Bernard (one boy – singular).
- A term's work is the work connected with, or possessed by, the term (one term – singular).

When the possessor noun is plural the apostrophe goes after the s:

- The girls' changing room is the changing room used, or possessed, by the girls (more than one girl – plural).
- Three years' effort is an effort lasting, or possessed by, three years (more than one year – plural).

Take care with words which already end in s or ss in their singular or plural form. Exactly the same rules apply:

- the duchess's dress (singular)
- three actresses' autographs (plural)
- Brahms's first symphony (singular)
- Mr Watts's class (singular).

Note that plural nouns which do not end in s – such as children and women – behave as if they were singular and take an apostrophe before the s when they are possessive. For example:

- working men's club
- children's games.

Omission

The apostrophe may also stand in place of missing letters in contracted words such as:

- wouldn't (would not)
- o'clock (of the clock)

- shan't (shall not)

- C'bury (Canterbury – on road signs)

- it's (it is or it has).

> Be particularly careful with **its** (which means belonging to it) and **it's** (which means it is or it has). Predictive text unhelpfully tends to assume that the writer always means *it's* so look closely at what you are typing.

Learn this example as part of your revision:
- It's a pity that our classroom has its door so close to the street.

Not using the apostrophe

Getting the apostrophe right is partly the art of knowing when *not* to use one.

An s at the end of a word usually shows that it is a plural noun and does not need an apostrophe. For example:

- three towns

- four dogs

- two sticks.

Or that it is part of a verb, for example:

- he says

- she runs

- Paul sobs.

None of these needs an apostrophe.

 Exam tip

Remember that far more words do *not* need an apostrophe than need one. Do your best to learn how the apostrophe is used and get it right in your exam. But if in doubt leave it out. You will make fewer mistakes that way.

No apostrophe is needed anywhere in a sentence like this:
- All the boys in classes one, two and three enjoy basketball lessons but Jules Atkins insists that he prefers card games.

Capital (or upper case) letters

Every sentence should begin with a capital letter.

Most capital letters are larger than the other letters in a word – make the distinction clearly, especially when the two forms are the same, or a similar, shape, such as Cc, Ss and Kk.

Many capital letters are a different shape from the lower case letter, such as Mm or Dd. Some, like Pp and Jj, have a different position on the line. Pay attention to this so that the examiner does not think you are misusing capital letters. If it looks to someone who is unfamiliar with your writing as though you are failing to begin sentences and proper nouns with a capital letter you will lose marks.

You also normally need an upper case or capital letter:

- For all proper nouns. For example:

  - Estella Jones, Bridgewood Preparatory School, Bristol, River Dee, Tesco.

- At the beginning of the first line of most poetry. For example:

  - Slowly, silently now the moon

    Walks the night in her silver shoon.

- Usually for the first word inside inverted commas. For example:

  - Aisha said, 'And I'll come too,' when she saw us getting ready.

- For most initials and acronyms. For example:

  - NATO, RSPCA.

> Sometimes handwriting makes it difficult to tell whether a letter is lower or upper case (small or capital). Make sure your writing is not guilty of this. Get out of bad handwriting habits if you need to.

6.3 Grammar

Grammar is a big subject and you will by now probably have studied the details carefully in your English lessons.

This section cannot cover the whole of English grammar, but here are some important things to revise and remember.

Agreement of subject and verb

Every sentence has a subject. It may be one word such as 'I' or 'Katie'. It may be something more complex such as 'Mr Patterson, our popular and witty Year 8 teacher'.

The subject often comes at the beginning of the sentence, but it doesn't have to.

Not far from the subject of any sentence is a verb – the action performed by the subject or the state the subject is in.

The sentence may have other elements too, but a subject and a verb are the basic building bricks.

It is important to make sure that your subject and verb agree. A singular subject needs a singular verb. If the subject is plural then, of course, it needs a plural verb. This is pretty straightforward in sentences such as:

- I **danced**.

- Katie **shouted** at the top of her voice.

- Mr Patterson, our popular and witty year 8 teacher, **retires** this year.

  But be careful in sentences like this:

- The weather, the miserable surroundings and the poor facilities **were** all responsible for our unsuccessful holiday. (Plural subject: 'The weather, the miserable surroundings and the poor facilities')

- Everyone **is** here. (Singular subject 'everyone')

  Take care too with collective nouns. They are singular:

- The Labour Party **is** planning its next election campaign.

- The choir **is** waiting for its conductor.

- The pride of lions **sleeps** most of the day.

Note that these words are all singular and need singular verbs to agree with them:

- anybody
- everybody
- nobody
- anyone
- each

- everyone
- everything
- either
- neither
- none

For example:

- **Neither** of the men **was** guilty.
- We lost several tennis balls but **none was** found.
- **Each** of the twenty quizzes **was** harder than the one before.

Clauses and phrases

Clauses and phrases are groups of words within sentences.

A clause has a verb of its own. For example:

- A nurse **she had not seen before** came and sat on the edge of her bed.
- And I knew that one day **when I was bigger** I would become one of the top men.
- We were in a small room **which held nothing except a large grating in the stone floor**.

A clause usually adds extra detail to the main sentence, but if you remove it the sentence should still make sense. Try it with the examples above.

A phrase is two or more words used together in a sentence. It does not include a verb. It can be a word group of almost any shape. For example:

- We followed him **through the house** until we reached the kitchen.
- They had seen the film **earlier that evening**.
- **Given the choice** I like fantasy stories best.
- Simon set out **wearing full climbing gear**.
- **Ladies and gentlemen**, I have an announcement to make.

Remember that good sentences consist of varying patterns of clauses and phrases woven together.

Ten mistakes to avoid

Work through these – perhaps study one a day for a few minutes.

Then tick them off when you've practised and understood them.

1 I and me

Don't confuse **I** with **me** when you put it with another person.

I is usually the subject in the sentence or clause and **me** the object (direct or indirect). If in doubt remove the other person from the sentence and work out what you would write if you were using the pronoun on its own.

So, you should write:

- Jonathan and **I** played cricket. (**I** played cricket.)
- She gave him and **me** a telling off. (She gave **me** a telling off.)

- Good night from her and **me**. (Good night from **me**.)
- My twin sister and **I** are 12 years old. (**I** am 12 years old.)

> Me and Tony went fishing ... is *always* wrong.
>
> Dad gave Charlotte and I ten pounds each ... is *always* wrong.

2 Himself, herself, myself, yourself

Do not use **himself** or **herself**, or **myself** or **yourself**, as the subject (or part of the subject) of a sentence.

- Sarah and I have ... is correct.
- Sarah and myself have ... is *always* wrong.

3 Too, to and two

- I am **too** tall for these trousers. (too much of something)
- Alex wanted to come **too**. (as well)
- She ate **two** ice creams. (number)
- May I have permission **to** go **to** the school office? (all other uses)

> Learn this sentence to help you remember the differences between too, to and two:
>
> **Two** boys, **too** curious for their own good, ran **to** the cupboard **to** look inside.

4 Two words or one?

Strictly speaking, **all right** is two separate words: **all** and **right**. The form **alright** is often seen, and is similar to the forms **altogether** and **already**, but is considered bad form in formal writing.

You should, however, learn the difference between **all ready** and **already**.

In this example, **ready** is an adjective telling you more about 'we', and **all** is a separate adverb telling you more about 'ready':

- Are we **all ready** to go?

In this example, 'already' is an adverb meaning 'in good time':

- He has arrived **already**.

Remember that **thank you** is two words. So is **a lot**.

> Work out the difference in meaning between 'altogether' and 'all together'.

5 Less, few and fewer

Less refers to quantity. For example:

- less salt
- less rainfall
- less hope.

Fewer or **few** refer to a number. For example:

- fewer eggs
- few people
- few schools.

A quick way of remembering this is that if it's something you can count (eggs, people, houses) it is **few** or **fewer**. If you can't count it, use **less**. Or remember that fewer cars means less traffic.

> Some British supermarkets have a notice up saying 'Baskets containing fewer than eight items' – which is correct. Several other supermarkets get this wrong. Watch out for it. The more aware you are, the *fewer* mistakes you will make yourself.

6 Lie and lay
Learn that **to lie** is a verb meaning either to put oneself in a horizontal position or to tell untruths. For example:

- I lie on the bed when I am tired.

- I lie to get myself out of difficult situations.

  The past tense for the first meaning is **lay** or **have lain**.
  For example:

- I lay on the grass all day yesterday.

- I have lain on the grass all morning and now it's time for lunch.

> On Sundays (if you're lucky) you might enjoy a lie-in – and it is an error to call it anything else.

The untruth sense is easier. The past tense is **lied** or **have lied**. For example:
- I lied to him yesterday because I have always lied to him.

The verb **to lay** is used when the person carrying out the action (the verb's subject) is doing something to something else (technically known as a transitive verb). For example:
- You can lay eggs (if you happen to be a hen), bricks, carpets or tables.

  The past tense is **laid** or **have laid**. For example:

- freshly laid eggs

- well-laid table.

Remember we're dealing with three different verbs here. Make sure you understand the difference so that you don't muddle them up.

7 Only, and other adverbs
It is important to put the word **only** in the correct place in a sentence. Getting it wrong (as many people do) changes the meaning. Study these examples:

- Only we saw the play that afternoon. (No one else saw it.)

- We saw only the play that afternoon. (We didn't see anything else.)

- We only saw the play that afternoon. (We didn't, for example, read it or rehearse it.)

- We saw the play only that afternoon. (We saw it very recently.)

Take care with the positioning of other adverbs such as **even**, **always** and **often** too. These two sentences do not mean quite the same thing:

- We even went swimming.

- Even we went swimming.

The first sentence suggests that there were lots of interesting things to do including swimming.

The second implies that many people were swimming so, although it was unusual for us, we did too.

Compare these two sentences:

- She often went to the cinema on Fridays.

- She went to the cinema, often on Fridays.

The first sentence means that usually, every Friday, she went to the cinema. The second means that she frequently went to the cinema on various days of the week, often choosing Fridays.

8 Practice and practise

Practice with a 'c' is a noun:

- I must do some clarinet practice.

- Practice is important if you want to improve your tennis.

- Dr Ahmed's medical practice covered three villages.

Sometimes it behaves as if it were an adjective:

- The practice rooms are at the back of the music room.

- The hour before supper is cricket practice time.

Practise with an 's' is a verb:

- I must practise the clarinet.

- Practise your tennis if you want to improve.

- Dr Ahmed and his colleagues practise in three villages.

Use **advice** and **advise** to help you remember this. They are easier because they sound different. Say aloud:

- Here is my advice. (noun)

- We could try the advice centre. (adjective)

- I advise you to apologise. (verb)

- She advised me to come. (verb)

Licence/license and **prophecy/prophesy** follow the same pattern.

Be aware that in American English these words are always spelled with a 'c' even when they are verbs.

9 Subjects

If you use a phrase or a clause before the subject of your sentence take care that it does not clash with the subject.

For example, do not write the following (it means that you are a wet day!):

- Being a wet day, I stayed indoors.

You should write one of the following:

- It was a wet day so I stayed indoors.

- I stayed indoors because it was a wet day.

Do not write the following as it sounds as if Jake is about to take the assembly and then stops talking:

- Knowing he was ready to begin assembly Jake stopped talking and listened to the headmaster.

You should write:

- Jake stopped talking and listened to the headmaster who was ready to begin the assembly.

10 They're, their and there

They're is a short form of **they are**. For example:

- They're enjoying the sunshine.

  Their is a possessive pronoun. For example:

- The children eat their lunch at 12 o'clock.

  There can be an adverb. For example:

- We walked there in half an hour.

  There can also be a pronoun. For example:

- Put your bag there.

  Study this correct sentence:

- As soon as the boys arrive they're expected to put their bags in the lockers over there.

6.4 Spelling

You will have done a lot of work on spelling in English (and perhaps other) lessons over the years. Now, as you revise, it's just a matter of going over the words you know you are likely to get wrong and memorising them.

Once you have mastered a particular word you are unlikely ever to have a problem with it again. And it usually takes only a minute or two's concentration.

You could work with a partner, testing each other, or you might prefer to work alone. Practise writing the words. Don't spell them aloud. That is a different skill (and a bit more difficult for most people). In your exam you will need to write them so concentrate on that.

 Exam tip

Incorrect spelling creates a bad impression. Don't just avoid writing a word that you can't spell in an exam, however, as this is a rather lazy solution and it limits your vocabulary. It is much better to spend a little time learning any spellings you don't know. It will help you in other subjects as well as English.

You could arrange the words you need to learn in short lists of five or ten, and focus on one list per day.

On page 71, in alphabetical order, are some of the most commonly misspelt everyday words in English.

 Revision tip

Keep a notebook of words you usually get wrong or find difficult and include these in your revision.

Tick each word off if – or when – you are confident that you can spell it:

absence	condemn	humour	proceed
access	conscience	immediate	profession
accommodation	conscientious	independent	pursue
achieve	coolly	install	queue
across	deceive	instalment	receipt
address	definitely	irritable	receive
advantageous	desirable	knowledge	recommend
aerial	despair	leisure	repetition
analyse	development	library	restaurant
anxious	disappear	likeable	rhyme
arctic	disappoint	lovable	rhythm
argument	dissatisfy	maintenance	ridiculous
association	eerie	manageable	secretary
author	eligible	Mediterranean	separate
autumn	exaggerate	miscellaneous	sincerely
awkward	exceed	mischief	solemn
beautiful	except	mischievous	success
beginning	excessive	necessarily	thorough
benefited	exhilaration	necessary	truly
biscuit	forty	neighbour	vicious
business	fulfil	niece	weird
ceiling	gauge	ninety	wholly
changeable	grammatical	noticeable	wilfully
commit	guard	occur	yacht
committed	handkerchief	occurring	yield
committee	height	parallel	
comparison	holiday	possession	
conceit	humorous	procedure	

★ Make sure you know

- ★ The different word classes or 'parts of speech'.
- ★ The main punctuation marks used in English.
- ★ The main grammar points to revise.
- ★ The ten key grammatical errors to avoid.
- ★ How to spell some of the most commonly misspelt words.

Test yourself

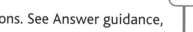

Make sure you can answer the following questions. See Answer guidance, page 84, for the answers.

1 What is a noun?
2 What is a verb?

3 What is an adjective?
4 What is an adverb?

5 What is a pronoun?
6 What is a preposition?

7 What is a conjunction?

8 Name the three punctuation marks which can end a sentence.

9 What are speech marks sometimes called?

10 Put the apostrophes in the correct place in this sentence:

Its a great shame that the tree has lost its leaves as its Dads favourite.

Answer guidance

Please remember that the suggestions here are just examples of the sorts of thing examiners are looking for. They are *not* the single, correct way of answering the questions. English is a very open-ended subject unlike, say, maths.

It might help to think of what you read here as 'notes' to help you to see what the questions, and the passages they relate to, mean and use this learning as part of your revision. In no sense is what follows here intended to be seen as the only correct answers. The text in italics provides guidance on how to allocate marks.

Chapter 2

1 Fiction

Level 1 (*The Day of the Triffids*)

1   The writer is surprised because he hears a steady tapping coming closer.

   One point from the first paragraph for 1 mark   (1)

2   The words are: 'Neatly dressed'; 'straightened up, a little defiantly'; and 'an exaggerated air of independence'.   (3)

   Three quotations needed for 3 marks

   The man is neatly dressed because, unlike all the others that are suddenly blind, he is used to dressing himself without seeing.

   He is defiant because he feels he is now more in charge as everyone is blind, but he has always been blind, so has an advantage.

   He has 'an exaggerated air of independence' because if everyone is blind, he is more free as he is used to being blind.   (6)

   1 mark for a short explanation of each quotation from the lines, 2 marks for a longer explanation

3   The writer tells us the young man is 'wearing a well-cut suit', which suggests he is used to dressing well and does so now even though he can't see a thing. Second, he knows how to make the best of a situation as he realises he has to find a way of getting food. So, he speaks to the woman and uses her child to confirm that there are 'Apples and fings in the shop'. He wouldn't normally steal but accepts that now he has to. (4)

   Either four short points or – better (as here) – two points (with quotations) explained in more detail

4   The woman has to look after her young child Mary, whom she comforts: "Go on, Mary. Tell the gentleman". Although the mother is blind and the child isn't, the child still relies on her mother. The mother also does not want to steal: "'But – ' she began". Even though she is hungry and the world has changed she does not want to do something she thinks is not right.   (4)

   Either four short points or – better (as here) – two points (with quotations) explained in more detail

5   'Why is it so quiet?'   (1)

1 mark

The 'normally blind' man is puzzled by the quiet. He knows it isn't night because he can feel the sun, so there should be lots of noise. He knows something is not right and draws attention to the unnatural quiet by asking his question.   (2)

1 mark for a brief explanation, 2 marks for a more detailed one

6   She says 'We didn't ought to take 'em'. This shows she feels that it is not right to steal, even if the world has suddenly changed and is no longer as it was. She still has a firm belief of what is right and what is wrong. When the man gives her an orange she says "But – ", showing she does not really want to eat the orange. Although she is hungry, she does not want to eat anything that has been stolen. She still does not want to break the law, even if there are no policemen to stop her.   (4)

Two quotations (for 1 mark each) with short explanations (each worth 1 mark) needed

Level 2 (*The Day of the Triffids*)

1   It is quiet with a great sense of everything having changed. The sound of the tapping getting louder and coming closer, at first unidentified, adds tension until the narrator (and the reader) realise what it is.   (3)

Three separate points about the atmosphere need to be made

2   He makes it clear that suddenly to be 'normally blind' is a reassuring advantage rather than a handicap. Vehicles have been abandoned (the inference is that no one can see to drive) so everything is quiet: a point reinforced by the description of the blind man tapping along which wouldn't normally be heard. He uses words such as 'groping' and 'collisions' to emphasise the fact that people trying to move about are likely to walk into each other. No one can get food in the conventional way so the ordinary rules of lawful behaviour are beginning to break down. The writer shows us an otherwise apparently respectable, well-dressed man breaking a shop window to steal fruit. The writer also presents us with the sad image of a mother being dependant on the eyes (and judgement) of her very young child – a poignant role reversal.   (4)

Either four brief points or two quotations (for 1 mark each) explained more fully (1 mark for each explanation)

3   The man has the qualities of jauntiness and confidence because he knows from long experience how to get about. Once he is told what has happened, and he has thought about it, he seems rather pleased – giving a 'short bitter laugh'– because he is now the one with the advantages. We are told that he walks away from the narrator 'with an exaggerated air of independence' and 'a little defiantly' which stresses his new-found cheerfulness. He has evidently resented being a victim of charity and sympathy in the past – as shown by his bitterness – and is now delighted that the rest of the population will need its 'patronage' for itself.   (6)

Three different quotations (for 1 mark each) and each quotation explained (1 mark for each explanation) needed

4   The 'woman who carried a small child' reminds the reader how difficult the situation is for ordinary people. The woman cannot see and they need food. This is a horrifying predicament. Also, Mary, the little girl, is very young. She whines, has to be carried and speaks childishly. Yet the child can see and the mother can't. The mother understands this but the child

evidently does not and the reader feels sympathy for them. Also, we can see that this child is going to be very valuable, not just to her mother but maybe also to others, which will make her vulnerable. That is why the writer presents the man they collide with who immediately uses the child's eyes to help him find food ('Look, Sonny, what's in there?') and although he shares it with the woman and child, others might not. (6)

Three different quotations (for 1 mark each) and each quotation explained (1 mark for each explanation) needed

5   The writer shows us what his five characters are like through what they say in this passage. We hear the exasperated – and slightly puzzled – self-reliance of the 'normally blind' man when he says to the narrator 'I've already been bumped into by God knows how many fools today.' He speaks assertively and almost angrily because he is used to being patronised, but he parts from the narrator fairly politely. Although this incident is slightly comic it also draws attention to the frightening strangeness which surrounds everybody in the passage. The conversation between 'the young man in the well-cut suit' and the mother and child makes us realise how desperate they are. All three are hungry. None of them would normally steal ('We didn't ought to take 'em. Not like this.' Says the woman) but the young man is able to rationalise and persuade: 'How else are you going to get food?' The writer uses speech in this passage to show us that these people come from different social classes. The woman and her child speak with a local accent in contrast to the young man who speaks to them. This reminds us that the disaster is affecting nearly everyone equally and breaking down barriers between groups. The dialogue also makes the action move faster and is more direct – like a play. These characters answer each other quickly and that too helps to reinforce their feeling of helplessness at the horrifying situation they find themselves in. (6)

Three different quotations (for 1 mark each) and each quotation explained (1 mark for each explanation) needed

2 Travel writing

Level 1 (*Under the Tuscan Sun*)

1   a)   She likes that 'they look like black-ink hieroglyphs' and that they can navigate by the stars. (2)

Two different points for 2 marks

   b)   They are handmade tools and one of them is like an elegant little sculpture. (2)

Two different points for 2 marks

2   'usual homes in dusty corners' and 'I trap them in a jar and take them outside.' (2)

Two different quotations about nature for 2 marks

The writer does not seem to mind that scorpions are in dusty corners and sees this as their natural home, as though they have just as much right to be there as she does. She seems to be at ease with nature.

That she feels at ease with nature and creepy-crawlies is shown by the fact that she does not kill the scorpions, which could be dangerous, and is not scared of them either, as a lot of people would be. She tries to get them out of the way and seems to do it almost as though she cares for the scorpions. (4)

1 mark for a brief explanation, 2 marks for a more detailed one of each quotation mentioned above

3 The local people ask 'How much did you pay for the house?' They think all Americans are rich and want to know how much money they paid for such an old house. They probably think it will be too much, showing the foreigners are a bit mad.

One person remembers that 'an artist from Naples lived there'. This shows the house has been empty for a long time and the writer wants us to know they are taking over a house that none of the local people wanted.   (4)

Two quotations (for 1 mark each) with explanations (each worth 1 mark) needed

4 'rusted pans, newspapers from 1958, wire, paint cans, debris' and 'an ugly red bed that we cannot figure out how to get down the narrow back stairs'.   (2)

1 mark per quotation

The list shows us that there are many things in the house that the writer has to clear out. The things listed are all useless, so it shows that the house is full of useless things that need to be thrown away.

Although the house should be empty, the previous owner has left a bed in one room that looks impossible to get out. They obviously found it too difficult to get rid of the bed, so they left it in the house, showing that no-one really cared for it and it is more rubbish tip than house. (4)

1 mark for a short explanation of the quotations mentioned above, 2 marks for a more detailed one

5 They have to bring water from the bathroom to the kitchen, which is not what they would be used to. Also, they do not have kitchen tables, but use two planks instead, which does not seem to bother them. They only have very few pots and pans and spoons in the kitchen, which is different to what they were used to. They cook pasta and eat a lot, because the work makes them hungry, and they fall asleep immediately, which they might not have done beforehand.   (5)

Five short points

Level 2 (*Under the Tuscan Sun*)

1 She enjoys the way they are shaped like 'hieroglyphs'. She admires their ability to navigate by the stars even when indoors.   (2)

Two separate points about the scorpions

2 The tools in the outhouses show how life was in the past. One is a tool for trimming grapes. Another is an old-fashioned container for hot coals for warming beds on damp, cold nights.   (2)

Two separate points about the tools

3 The writer, who admires 'the beauty of scorpions', is comfortable with nature and interested in it. Rather than being frightened of the minibeasts in her house and trying aggressively to get rid of them she observes them closely. She respectfully traps the scorpions in a jar and takes them outside rather than killing them and seems quite sorry if she accidentally sucks some into the vacuum cleaner. Even the scorpion in the bidet or the white one from her pillow doesn't faze her much. Also she notices 'Whole eco-systems of spiders and scorpions' in her house but doesn't seem to mind that they come straight back when she tries to get rid of them.   (4)

4   The writer and her husband are foreigners. The local people 'pause in the road and look up at all the mad activity' because they find it odd that Mayes and Ed should want to live in this old house which needs so much work doing to it. Neighbours pass by and try to strike up conversations because they're curious. Mayes conveys this by mentioning them and including some of what they say. Also, to the locals, the two 'incomers' would have seemed eccentric and Mayes sees things from the onlookers' point of view with her description: 'the car trunk full of bottles, mattress flying, me screaming as a scorpion falls down my shirt when I sweep the stone walls of the stall, Ed wielding a grim-reaper scythe through the weeds.' The cultural differences are there too. She is surprised at the casual enquiry about the house price from complete strangers.   (4)

5   Mayes contrasts shopping in a fancy American cookware shop 'Williams-Sonoma', which in America she treats as a 'toy store', with the simplicity of cooking pasta with wooden spoons and a few other basic kitchen tools in her 'surprisingly manageable kitchen' despite its lack of modern fittings and running hot water. She has even grown used to bringing 'hot water from the bathroom in a plastic laundry pan'. Also, she remembers seeing the house before they bought it full of 'fanciful iron beds with painted medallions of Mary and shepherds holding lambs, wormy chests of drawers with marble tops, cribs, foxed mirrors, cradles, boxes, and lugubrious bleeding-heart religious pictures of the Crucifixion' but now, in stark contrast, it contains only scorpions, spiders and rubbish.   (6)

6   They are very busy and physically active – becoming dry and thirsty, 'as parched as the hills around us'. They are gently modernising the kitchen – with a new fridge and stove – but have adapted to the fairly primitive arrangements for hot water which has to be carried by hand from the bathroom. They are happy to make do with an improvised kitchen work surface consisting of a trestle arrangement and the basic implements for cooking. Because they are working so hard – 'we haul and scrub' – and for so long each day they sleep well and have very healthy appetites. 'After long work, we eat everything in sight then tumble like field hands into bed,' she says. We infer, because she's telling us all this, that their lives, activity levels and diet in America would have been very different.   (7)

3 Biography/autobiographical writing

Level 1 (*Anita and Me*)

1   She wears saris and formal Indian suits.   (2)

She dresses like this because she sees it as part of the English people's education. It is her duty to show the English people that she can wear clothes like that and look glamorous.   (2)

2 The narrator obviously gets on well with her mother, because they have 'very special shopping outings' together. If you are doing something with someone else you would only call that 'special' if you like the other person. Also, the fact that they do shopping together shows they are close.

But the narrator doesn't agree with how her mother dresses, as she says 'she would get fewer stares and whispers'. The narrator is obviously not happy that people are staring at her mother and she thinks her mother should wear normal clothes so they don't. So here, the two disagree. (4)

Two quotations (for 1 mark each) with explanations (each worth 1 mark) needed

3 The parents obviously share secrets as they talk in 'soft whispers', showing they don't want the narrator to hear and that they work and plan things together that they don't want their daughter to hear.

They defend each other, so when the narrator says 'She won't' and starts to make fun of her mother, the father steps in and makes her be quiet. The father stands up for his wife, showing they are close.

The father obviously takes care of the mother as he keeps looking at the 'mother's face'. (5)

Either five short points or fewer, with 2 marks for each quotation with explanation; the three points mentioned in the question must be dealt with

4 The narrator plays with her food and the sausage 'suddenly' shoots into her mouth. This is funny as it's almost like the hot-dog is a gun, but a strange one. Being shot by a sausage is ridiculous.

The fact that she is in shock and pain, but the parents don't notice as they are 'engrossed', is also funny. You would expect parents to care for their children, but here, when she is possibly really dying, the parents don't seem to notice, although it's happening right behind them.

Although she feels she might die, the narrator is 'thrilled'. Normally no-one is excited to die, so the fact that she writes that she is makes us realise she is not going to die and she is just making it all sound bigger than it is, which is funny, as choking on a sausage would be a silly way to die. (6)

Three different quotations (1 mark per quotation) and each quotation explained (1 mark for each explanation) needed

5 The narrator is not very respectful to her mother, as she makes fun of her: 'I can make this cheaper at home'. Although she is quiet when her father tells her off, she doesn't seem to feel her mother is a person that she must always respect. (6)

She loves food, as she is 'licking the tomato sauce off my fingertips'. She eats a hotdog after the rum baba, so obviously likes eating food. The food she eats is not very healthy, so she obviously likes junk food and eating a large amount rather than good things.

She writes in detail and uses nice words, like 'vibrating thin silks'. The narrator makes pictures come to life by choosing more precise words to show how cloth moves. She likes to use detail to bring her story to life.

Three different quotations (1 mark per quotation) and each quotation explained (1 mark for each explanation) needed (6)

Level 2 (*Anita and Me*)

1 a) She is an educated woman (a teacher) and wants to give an impression of Indian women which helps to make other British

people see them as acceptable. For her, that means wearing traditional Indian dress elegantly without looking gaudy. (2)

Two points needed

b) The narrator is impatient with this view and thinks her mother would do better to wear the ordinary British clothes she wears to school. There is a note of exasperated sarcasm in her observation that her mother sees 'English people's education' as 'her duty'. (2)

Two points needed

2 In the tense scene in the café the narrator gives a humorous account of her younger self tucking cheerfully into a 'rum baba' (it's her birthday) while her mother refuses to eat anything. Syal makes it clear that at the time the narrator doesn't really know what is upsetting her mother who is unusually quiet, but she is irritated by her mother's refusal to join in by having a cake. The tension is suggested in the contrast between the narrator's enjoyment of her cake and her mother's attitude to eating out. We don't hear the mother speak in this passage which helps to evoke a sense of her being upset and her daughter's being impervious to it. The narrator assumes – and rudely spells it out – that her mother objects to paying for an expensive, inferior shop-bought cake and trots out some of her mother's usual arguments ('I can make this cheaper at home'). We infer from this that the writer is often told by her mother that English food is overpriced and unpleasant and that she can make better at home. The narrator, who is eating an ordinary British cake, clearly finds this infuriating and would simply like to conform to British ways. (4)

Either two quotations (1 mark per quotation) explained more fully (1 mark for each explanation) or four points

3 The narrator's father is concerned about his wife who seems to be upset ('no light in her face') and is being kind to her in the café by trying to persuade her to have something to eat that he knows she likes – a meringue. He seems to be kind and loving. Also, we see him very angry with his daughter because of her rude outburst against her mother – from which we can deduce that he and his wife have a strong supportive relationship. But then the mother silently asks the father not to be so hard on his daughter by covering the child's hand and shaking her head at her husband. It is clear that the couple are well attuned to each other. Also, once the three of them are in the car, he and his wife talk to each other softly and exclude their daughter. The word 'again' is significant. The narrator makes it clear that there is some ongoing issue which she doesn't, child as she is, understand. It is obvious too that the mother is in tears ('seemed to wipe something from her face') in the front of the car, although her daughter is oblivious. (5)

Either five short points or fewer, with 2 marks for each quotation with explanation

4 The final paragraph includes words such as 'squeezed', 'shot' and 'lodged', which are witty overstatements in this context so it is comic.

The narrator's father has bought her a compensatory hot dog because it's her birthday and, gently reprimanded by his wife, he regrets telling her off. When a piece of sausage gets stuck in her throat she briefly thinks she's going to die – which seems glamorous and exciting. 'I felt thrilled. It was so dramatic,' she says.

The contrast to the glamour comes as a comic anti-climax. She can't get the attention of her preoccupied parents because she 'could not spell sausage'.

Set against this is the anxious, whispered conversation ('They were still talking, engrossed') going on between her impervious parents in the front of the car. Something serious is distressing them and that heightens the situation comedy of their daughter in the back choking on something as mundane as a lump of sausage. (6)

Three different quotations (1 mark per quotation) and each quotation explained (1 mark for each explanation) needed

5   The narrator – an adult looking back, obviously – recalls and presents herself as a rather self-absorbed child. She is annoyed that on her birthday her parents are preoccupied about something else and 'they were leaving me out again'. The irritation and frustration with her mother is clearly ongoing. The mother says none of the things attributed to her while the family is in the café. The narrator is regurgitating what she so often hears her mother say.

She is clearly keen on food. She evokes the exact consistency of the rum baba's 'spongy belly' and we can almost taste the tomato sauce on the hot dog and hear her singing (to draw attention from her parents?) 'between slurps'. On the other hand, she is aware that her mother is upset although she chooses to ignore it. She notices her father's eyes anxiously flicking towards his wife while he is driving, having also seen, but not apparently recognised, her mother shedding a tear. The adult narrator wants us to see 'past' her child self and work out with her, as readers, what was really going on. The narrator is also a humorist and, with hindsight, can see the funny side of the events she's remembering. (6)

Three different quotations (1 mark per quotation) and each quotation explained (1 mark for each explanation) needed

4 Drama

Level 1 (*War Horse*)

1   a)   Nicholls wants Joey to get used to the sound of gunfire. (1)

One point for 1 mark

b)   Joey 'reacts' so is showing he is nervous in some way. (1)

One point for 1 mark

2   a)   He wants all shiny things to be dull so they don't alert the enemy by flashing in the sun. (1)

One point for 1 mark

b)   Nicholls says 'I know, Warren, after all that hard work', which shows Ned is not pleased. (1)

One quotation for 1 mark

3   'Two proud animals' and 'Joey and Topthorn are only interested in each other.' (2)

1 mark for each quotation

'Two proud animals' tells us that both Joey and Topthorn see themselves as the leader and will not easily give in to the other. When they are put together it is not clear who will come out on top.

The two horses 'are only interested in each other' shows us that the horses are starting to sort out their differences. They are getting to know one another, as though this is something they must do before they can focus on anything else. (4)

1 mark for a short explanation of the quotations mentioned above, 2 marks for a more detailed one

4 Stewart is excited about going into battle. He knows from his uncle that the British cavalry charge is fearful and he expects them to cut a swathe through the Germans. (3)

Three points needed

5 Nicholls is the most senior officer and he gives the commands and sees that everything is done. He is not sure about the war and seems thoughtful.

Stewart is an officer under Nicholls. He is keen to go to war, although he has never experienced it.

Ned Warren is a trooper and carries out orders, but does not say much. (6)

Two points per person needed for full marks (1 mark per point made)

6 'You'll be all right, won't you boys?' and 'You think I'll be up to it?' (2)

1 mark per quotation

Everyone in this scene is feeling tense because they are thinking about what they face tomorrow when they will have to be 'warlike and violent'. It sums up the nervousness and fear they are all feeling. Nicholls is reflecting on the calm, peaceful horses and imagining a nightmare world in which they too become violent like men.

All of them know, without spelling it out, that 'men tend to go to pieces' in battle – whichever side they are on – although Stewart applies it only to the Germans here. It underlines the terror they are dealing with and the horror they face. They have to be brave, obviously, but thinking about it is making them tense. Stewart talks of how they will 'cut a swathe through Fritz' although, as Nicholls tells him, he will have to find out for himself just what it's like to be in a battle. (4)

1 mark for a short explanation of the quotations mentioned above, 2 marks for a more detailed one

Level 2 (*War Horse*)

1 Nicholls is getting Joey used to very loud, close noise and to the smell of gunfire so that when he is in battle he won't panic. (1)

One point for 1 mark

The noise of the guns clearly needs to be very loud so there should be no other sound. The people puppeting Joey should make him jump and flinch but less for each gun shot as he gradually becomes 'desensitised'. (2)

1 mark for short explanation, 2 marks for longer explanation

2 Nicholls doesn't want his men to have anything shiny on their uniforms which might glint in the sun and attract enemy attention. (1)

One point for 1 mark

He says 'I know, Warren, after all that hard work' which suggests that Ned looks surprised, or even annoyed, because soldiers are normally expected to spend a lot of time polishing their boots, buckles and other equipment. (2)

1 mark for short explanation, 2 marks for longer explanation

3 Joey is the horse Nicholls is working with while Captain Stewart is using Topthorn. Both are 'proud animals'. Joey seems to be slightly faster when they practise charging because Nicholls gently ribs the captain about being behind and Stewart says 'We were breathing right down your neck, as you well know.' The two horses are interested in each other – when they are brought together at the end of the scene they make that clear although they evidently don't yet know each other well. Stewart tells Nicholls that they are 'snippy' with each other, which from the context seems to mean 'wary' and trying to work out which of them is dominant. (4)

Two quotations (1 mark per quotation) explained more fully (1 mark for each explanation)

4 Stewart is partly excited and partly nervous. He wants to 'cut a swathe through Fritz' by which he means to attack the Germans and beat them. He is also thinking about stories he's heard from his uncle who says that 'men tend to go to pieces when our cavalry bear down on them.' So he believes that men – the enemy – sometimes fall apart when they see a British cavalry charge. He speaks with courage and bravado but there's also a sense that he doesn't really know what to expect. We get a sense that Stewart's feelings are mixed. (4)

Two quotations (1 mark per quotation) explained more fully (1 mark for each explanation)

5 The playwright makes it clear that these men hold different army ranks. He uses speech, action and silence to make the differences clear.

Nicholls is evidently the most senior – he is shown giving the orders and takes charge of the conversation assertively in response to Stewart's reference to his uncle: 'every generation has to discover things for themselves' he says firmly (but ungrammatically). He is also courteous and respectful: 'not casting aspersions on your uncle's experience'.

Stewart is a lower-ranking officer, a captain – the playwright has Nicholls ask him about his troop to make this clear. We infer that, unlike Nicholls, he has not been into battle before because he is speculating about the expected conflict the next day. The playwright shows him talking excitedly and gushingly about what he hopes to do to the Germans: 'he won't know what's hit him. He'll wish he'd never been born' which is the playwright's way of showing Stewart's nervousness.

Ned is not an officer but a trooper and may be younger (the playwright uses his first name). He takes instructions about practical things such as polishing and doesn't speak other than to acknowledge orders. He says little but his function here is to remind the reader/theatre audience that as well as officers such as Stewart and Nicholls there are many thousands of ordinary men, many of them very young like Ned. (5)

One to two points per person needed (1 mark per point), up to a maximum of 5 marks

6 None of these men should seem at all relaxed. All their thoughts are focused on what they will face when they arrive in France to 'put a swathe through Fritz'. The 'rapid rounds' being fired near Joey at the beginning should be against a background of quiet. Just as Joey reacts, so should the audience.

The actors, now it is clear that they're 'posted to France' should show their tension in their movements, perhaps by pacing about, clenching their hands or drumming their fingers, although each is desperate not to show the others how tense he is feeling.

Nicholls speaks gently to Joey: 'Good boy. This is a gun. The smell is cordite. Try again.' He has to appear calm to Ned and Stewart because he is the most senior, but the actor should make us sense that beneath the surface he is apprehensive when he says, for example 'I was pleased with the practice charge today.' Unlike Stewart, and presumably Ned, Nicholls has experienced frontline war before so has more reason to be frightened than the others, although they too are nervous. And the horses will sense this so the puppeteers manipulating them should make the animals jumpy too.   (6)

Three different quotations (1 mark per quotation) and each quotation explained (1 mark for each explanation) needed

Chapter 3

Level 1 ('Sunken Evening')

1   The starlings 'stow their mussel shells' meaning they are settling for the night.   (1)

One point for 1 mark

2   The typist is 'trapped by telephones' meaning he can't leave his place as he has to answer telephones the whole time. He does not want to be doing this, though, as he is staring at the sky.   (2)

1 mark for short explanation, 2 marks for longer explanation

An oyster is a shellfish that has a hard shell, but is soft inside and can contain a pearl. The poet perhaps looks quite dull on the outside, but he is obviously kind inside.   (2)

1 mark for short explanation, 2 marks for longer explanation

3   'feathered fish' and 'lobster-buses'   (2)

1 mark per quotation

Fish are underwater animals, but they are not feathered, birds are. The poet is mixing up fish and birds as both fly or swim in the blue and seem to float in the sky or ocean. They are very similar.

Buses in London are bright red, as a lobster is. A bus is also quite chunky and the metal around it is almost like armour. The lobster has armour around it and looks quite large and solid and heavy, too.   (4)

1 mark for a short explanation of the quotations mentioned above, 2 marks for a more detailed one

4   In the last verse it becomes dark 'the slow night' comes. The poem so far has described the day and all the things that happen in the city during the day. Now, in the last stanza, night falls, bringing a change.

At the end of the day all the people travel 'homeward'. During the day the city was full of people, but now, with the dark they all go back to their different lives outside of the city.   (4)

Either two quotations (for 1 mark each) with explanations (each worth 1 mark) or four shorter points

5   'The Mall', 'lobster-buses' and 'pigeons feed'   (3)

1 mark per point

The Mall is a place in London and London buses are red, like lobsters. Also, London is full of pigeons.   (2)

1 mark per point

6   A city is a very busy place during the day, much like an underwater scene can be: there are lots of birds in a city, and the sea around a reef has many fish. There are also many different animals in the sea and a city, like the 'lobster-buses' or the 'prawn-blue pigeons'. There seems to be a lot going on both underwater and in a city, so the comparison is good. The 'tides' mentioned at the end also fit well, as these are like crowds of people moving backwards and forwards, much like waves do.   (5)

Either five short points or fewer, with 2 marks for each quotation with explanation

Level 2 ('Sunken Evening')

1   The starlings are flying in and out of the hollows and spaces in the walls of the church, carrying bits and pieces. The poet imagines them bringing metaphorical mussel shells to a wreck as if the birds were underwater creatures. Their feathers have a multi-coloured sheen which reminds the poet of the shiny phosphorescence sometimes seen on the surface of the sea.   (3)

1 mark per point

2   The whole poem is an extended metaphor in which the poet compares the city with the sea. Because the light is green it is like an underwater scene. In this metaphor the birds are 'feathered fish' (a good expression because of the alliteration which makes them sound very light and fluttery). The slow (red) buses are compared with lobsters and the blue-ish grey pigeons with prawns. The fountains in the square, with their spraying water, look like waterweed and the wide road nearby has 'sandy grottoes'. The church is described as a wreck (perhaps it was damaged – maybe in a war) with a long shape which resembles the hull of a ship.   (4)

Two quotations (1 mark per quotation) explained more fully (1 mark for each explanation)

3   The typist has to stay at her desk because she must answer the telephone. It is as if she were trapped on the sea bed so she gazes longingly toward the surface of the water and the sky because that would be freedom. All she can see is bubbles which symbolise something very fragile which soon disappears. The poet is comparing himself with an unattractive looking oyster with a hard grey crusty shell but with something precious and beautiful – the poem – inside, like an oyster's pearl.   (4)

Either two quotations (1 mark per quotation) explained more fully (1 mark for each explanation) or four short points

4   a)   The last verse hangs on its first word – the adverb 'Till' – which is a turning point to show that the poem is about to move off in a different direction. It is now dark and time for the workers to go home.   (1)

1 mark per point

   b)   The poet imagines the tide going out as the city empties so that the workers are washed out of the deep sea and stranded. Night, which 'trawls its heavy net', is personified as a fisherman dragging the workers like fish through shallow waters towards their homes on the outskirts of the city. They are then stranded by the tide in their suburbs.   (2)

1 mark per point

5   The poem is obviously set in a city, as the first line mentions a 'city square'. While other areas where people live may have features like

fountains and churches, the fact that the poem specifically mentions a 'city' square suggests it is set in a larger urban area. The poem also talks about red 'lobster-buses'. While buses can be seen all over the country they are not usually red, unless they are in larger cities. Most famous of all are the London red buses, so the poem could be set in London. Finally, the poem refers to a place called 'the Mall'. The fact that 'Mall' has a capital letter shows it is an actual location and not an ordinary shopping mall, suggesting that the poem is set in a well-known city, probably London. (6)

Three different quotations (1 mark per quotation) and each quotation explained (1 mark for each explanation) needed

6   This poem presents London at dusk and compares its emptying and gradual quietening with the tide going out. Verbs such as 'floods' and 'trawls' and nouns such as 'squalls', 'weed' and 'bubbles' help to sustain the metaphor which runs right through the poem to create an imaginative picture. The poet's rhyme scheme in each stanza uses half rhymes ('fish'/'splash', 'run'/'Surbiton') as well as full rhymes ('dry'/'sky', 'fret'/'net') giving the poem a fluid feel which complements the comparison of crowds rushing to waves. The occasional use of internal rhyme within stanzas ('trawls'/'hauls', 'bell'/ 'shells') adds to this effect. So does the use of alliteration in, for example, 'fowl and feathered fish', 'typist, trapped by telephones'. The rhythm supports the comparison of people leaving the city with waves and the tide. The poet mixes polysyllables with monosyllables ('phosphorescent starlings', 'tide and fret') to build the rhythm of moving water. Overall I find this quite moving poem makes successful use of many techniques which, together, form a satisfying and imaginative comparison of commuters with the changing sea. (5)

Either five short points or fewer, with 2 marks for each quotation with explanation

Chapter 6

Test yourself

1   A noun is a naming word.

2   A verb is an action or 'being' word.

3   An adjective is a describing word which qualifies or modifies a noun.

4   An adverb is a describing word which qualifies or modifies a verb.

5   A pronoun stands in the place of a noun.

6   A preposition tells you the position of something in relation to something else.

7   A conjunction is a joining word.

8   A full stop, question mark or exclamation mark can end a sentence.

9   Speech marks are sometimes called inverted commas or quotation marks.

10   It's a great shame that the tree has lost its leaves as it's Dad's favourite.